GREAT OCEAN ROAD
AND **GRAMPIANS**

AUSTRALIA'S TOP TOURING REGIONS

www.gregorys-online.com

www.planbooktravel.com

Produced and published in Australia by Gregory's Publishing Company
(a division of Universal Publishers Pty Ltd) ABN 83 000 087 132
and **Digitravel Publishing Pty Ltd** (trading as PlanBookTravel) ABN 81 106 431 672

Marketed and distributed by:
Universal Publishers Pty Ltd

New South Wales:
1 Waterloo Road, Macquarie Park 2113
Ph: (02) 9857 3700 Fax: (02) 9888 9850

Queensland:
1 Manning Street, South Brisbane 4101
Ph: (07) 3844 1051 Fax: (07) 3844 4637

South Australia:
Freecall: 1800 021 987

Victoria:
585 Burwood Road, Hawthorn 3122
Ph: (03) 9818 4455 Fax: (03) 9818 6123

Western Australia:
38a Walters Drive, Osborne Park 6017
Ph: (08) 9244 2488 Fax: (08) 9244 2554

International distribution
Ph: +61 2 9857 3700 Fax: +61 2 9888 9850

All rights reserved. PlanBookTravel is the owner of the copyright of all text (except 'Mahogany Ship') and maps in this publication. Other than as permitted by the Copyright Act, no part of this publication may be reproduced, copied or transmitted, in any form or by any means (electronic, mechanical, microcopying, photocopying, recording, storage in a retrieval system or otherwise), without the prior written consent of Gregory's Publishing Company and Digitravel Publishing Pty Ltd. Universal Publishers Pty Ltd and Digitravel Publishing Pty Ltd will vigorously pursue any breach of its copyright.

Great Ocean Road and Grampians
ISBN 0 7319 1960 2

1st edition 2006

Design: PlanBookTravel (www.planbooktravel.com)
Text (except 'Mahogany Ship') and Maps: ©PlanBookTravel (www.planbooktravel.com)
Text 'Mahogany Ship' © Tony Fawcett

Printed: Craft Print Pte Ltd

Disclaimer
The publishers disclaim any responsibility or duty of care towards any person for loss or damage suffered from any use of this guide for whatever purpose and in whatever manner. While considerable care has been taken by the publishers in researching and compiling the guide, the author and publisher accept no responsibility for errors or omissions. No person should rely upon this guide for the purpose of making any business, investment or real estate decision.

The representation on any maps of any road or track is not necessarily evidence of public right of way. Third parties who provide information to the publishers concerning roads and other matters do not assert or imply to the publishers that such information is complete, accurate or current or that any of the proposals of any body will eventuate and, accordingly, the publishers makes no such assertions or implications.

www.planbooktravel.com

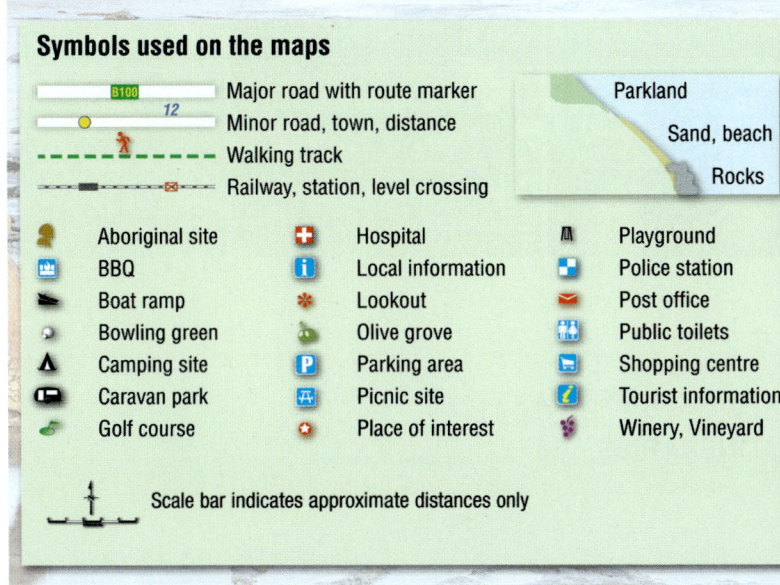

Symbols used on the maps

B100	Major road with route marker
12	Minor road, town, distance
- - - 🚶 - - -	Walking track
▬▬■▬▬⊠▬▬	Railway, station, level crossing

Parkland
Sand, beach
Rocks

👤	Aboriginal site	✚	Hospital	🎠	Playground
	BBQ	ℹ️	Local information		Police station
	Boat ramp	✳️	Lookout	✉️	Post office
	Bowling green		Olive grove	🚻	Public toilets
▲	Camping site	🅿️	Parking area	🛒	Shopping centre
	Caravan park		Picnic site		Tourist information
	Golf course		Place of interest	🍇	Winery, Vineyard

Scale bar indicates approximate distances only

GREAT OCEAN ROAD AND GRAMPIANS

Photographic Acknowledgments:
Jeremy Baird: pp.4 (T: left, 2nd left, right), 16, 17, 19, 21, 22, 24, 28, 32, 34, 37, 38, 51
Michael Doomernik: pp.58, 115 (B)
Tony Fawcett: pp.102, 103
Glenelg Shire Council: pp.110 (T), 111, 113, 114, 115 (T), 116–117
Great Southern Destinations Marketing (GDSM): pp.13, 39, 82, 83
Natural Wanders: pp.47, 110 (B), 112, 142, 143 (B)
Southern Grampians Shire Council: pp.129, 130, 131, 139, 140, 141, 143 (T)
Tourism Victoria: pp.1, 2–3, 4 (T 2nd right), 5, 6–7, 11, 12 (B), 14, 18, 20, 27, 29, 30, 35, 40, 42, 43, 44, 46, 48, 52, 53, 54, 56, 57, 60, 62, 67, 68, 70, 72, 73, 74, 75, 76, 86, 90, 99, 101, 104, 106 (B), 107, 118–119, 120, 123, 124, 126, 127, 128, 132, 133, 134, 135, 136, 137, 138, 144, 145, 146
Warrnambool City Council: pp.78, 85, 91, 92, 93, 94, 95, 96, 97, 98 (B)
Glen Watson: pp.10, 12 (T), 15, 66, 79, 80, 84, 87, 88, 89, 98 (T), 100, 106 (T), 108, 109

CONTENTS

GREAT OCEAN ROAD   6
GREAT OCEAN ROAD 2–3 DAY ITINERARIES   14
GREAT OCEAN ROAD 3–5 DAY ITINERARIES   16
GEELONG TO TORQUAY   18
GEELONG   20
TORQUAY TO LORNE   30
TORQUAY   32
HIGHLIGHTS BETWEEN TORQUAY AND ANGLESEA   38
ANGLESEA   40
SURF COAST WALK   44
HIGHLIGHTS BETWEEN ANGLESEA AND AIREYS INLET   46
AIREYS INLET   48
ANGAHOOK-LORNE STATE PARK   52
LORNE TO APOLLO BAY   54
LORNE   56
HIGHLIGHTS BETWEEN LORNE AND APOLLO BAY   64
APOLLO BAY TO PORT CAMPBELL   66
APOLLO BAY   68
THE OTWAYS   74
HIGHLIGHTS BETWEEN APOLLO BAY AND PORT CAMPBELL   76
PORT CAMPBELL TO WARRNAMBOOL   78
PORT CAMPBELL   80
SHIWRECKS   84
PORT CAMPBELL NATIONAL PARK   86

www.planbooktravel.com

HIGHLIGHTS BETWEEN PORT CAMPBELL
 AND WARRNAMBOOL   88
WARRNAMBOOL TO PORTLAND   90
WARRNAMBOOL   92
VOLCANO, WHALES & SHIPWRECKS   98
HIGHLIGHTS BETWEEN WARRNAMBOOL AND PORT FAIRY   100
MAHOGANY SHIP   102
PORT FAIRY   104
HIGHLIGHTS BETWEEN PORT FAIRY AND PORTLAND   110
PORTLAND   112
HIGHLIGHTS BETWEEN PORTLAND AND MOUNT GAMBIER   116
THE GRAMPIANS   118
GRAMPIANS 2–3 DAY ITINERARIES   122
GRAMPIANS 3–5 DAY ITINERARIES   124
ARARAT   126
STAWELL   130
HALLS GAP   132
HALLS GAP WALKS AND DRIVES   136
WINE & OLIVES   140
ABORIGINAL CULTURE   142
DUNKELD   144
BEYOND DUNKELD   146
INDEX   148

GREAT OCEAN ROAD AND GRAMPIANS

GREAT OCEAN ROAD

GREAT OCEAN ROAD

APPROXIMATE DISTANCES:

- Geelong to Torquay 24km
- Torquay to Lorne 47km
- Lorne to Apollo Bay 45km
- Apollo Bay to Port Campbell 96km
- Port Campbell to Warrnambool 66km
- Warrnambool to Portland 102km

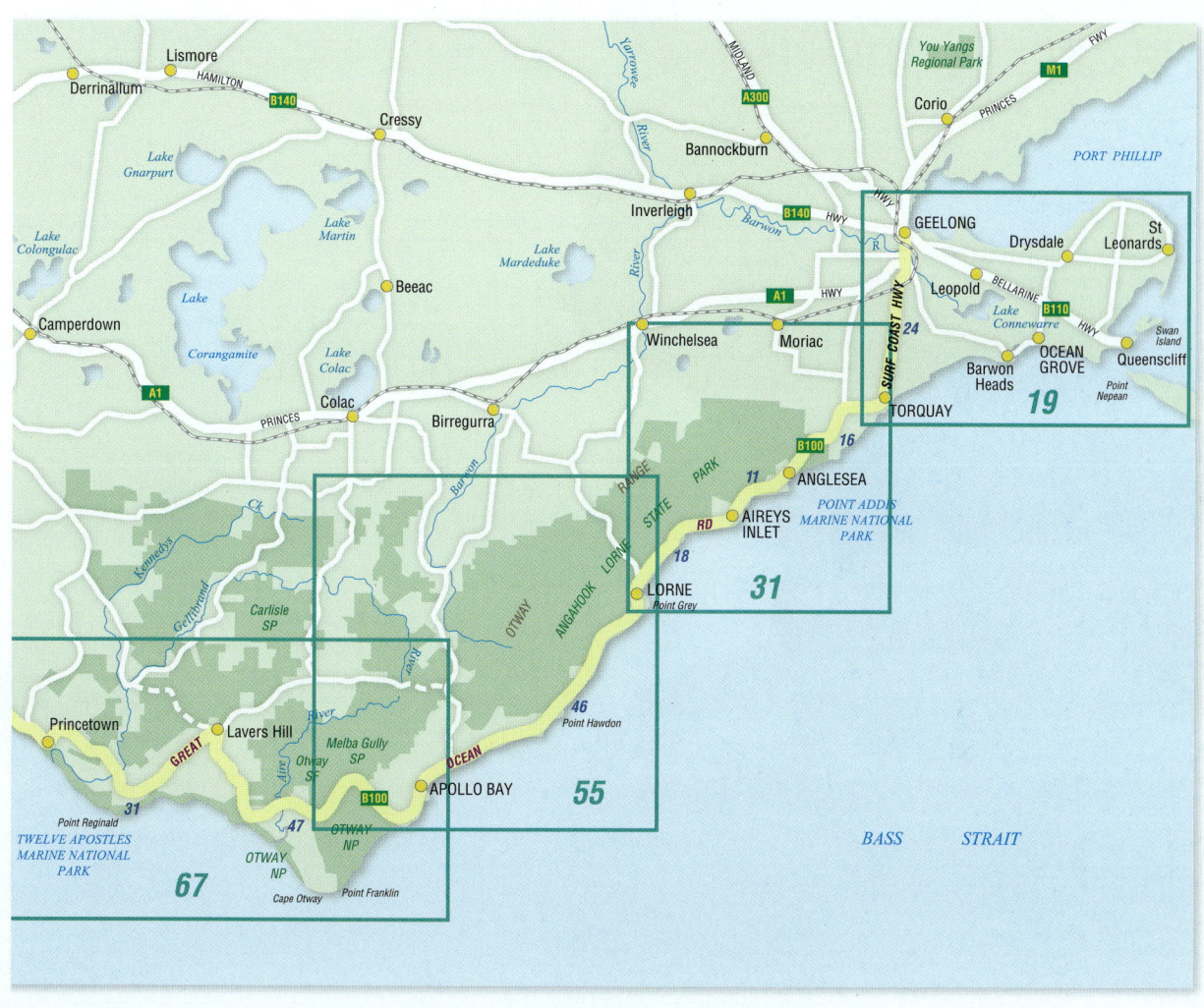

GREAT OCEAN ROAD

Clinging to Victoria's magnificent south-west coast, the Great Ocean Road follows a circuitous route around the coastline for 300km from Torquay to Warrnambool.

Begun in 1919 and finished in 1932, this tourism icon was built by returned WWI soldiers using only picks and shovels; the road is dedicated to the memory of their comrades killed in the war. Its completion ended a long history of isolation, when the only link to Melbourne and the western coastal communities was by sea. Today, the Great Ocean Road offers other benefits, particularly sightseeing.

The road traverses cliff edges, rugged headlands, undulating farmland, pristine beaches and wide river floodplains. In fact, the scenery changes so dramatically that you will experience three distinctly different sections of the road: the Surf Coast, the Otway Range and the Shipwreck Coast. Much of the route skirts, or passes through, some of Victoria's most spectacular state, national and marine parks, which offer the chance to get close to a variety of wildlife, from whales to koalas.

The journey begins in Geelong, Victoria's second largest city and gateway to the Surf Coast. Further south is the Bellarine Peninsula, known for its architecture, art, fine cool-climate wines and cuisine. Not far from the peninsula are the famous surf beaches of Torquay, including Bells Beach.

There's plenty of great surf and swimming beaches all along the road, like those at Anglesea, Aireys Inlet, Lorne, Wye River, Kennett River and Apollo Bay. Beyond Anglesea, the Great Ocean Road leaves the coast and winds its way into the lush forests of the Otway Range. Here you will be captivated by cool fern gullies, crystal-clear streams, thundering waterfalls and dense rainforest. At Cape Otway, the most southerly point of the road, stands Australia's oldest lighthouse. West of the imposing cliffs of Cape Otway stretches the treacherous Shipwreck Coast which continues as far as Port Fairy. Along this coast more than 80 ships were lost during the 1800s. If the Great Ocean Road is distinctive to this point, then between Port Campbell and Peterborough it becomes entirely unique.

Marvel at the remarkable rock formations of the Twelve Apostles, of which eight are left standing, and Loch Ard Gorge, natural phenomena that rival Uluru (Ayers Rock) and the Great Barrier Reef in their international appeal.

Beyond the Apostles lies Warrnambool, famous as an observation point for whale watching, especially during the calving season; then picturesque Port Fairy and the bustling harbour town of Portland. The latter was Victoria's first white settlement and its oldest town. Indeed, the Portland Maritime Discovery Centre is steeped in the rich history of the place. The centre exhibits a sperm whale skeleton, and the lifeboat that played such an heroic part in rescuing survivors of the *Admella* shipwreck in 1859. Portland is also the jumping off point or

GREAT OCEAN ROAD

MOORING AT PORT FAIRY

the finish line for the Great Southwest Walk, a 250km track favoured by long distance walkers

Pick any town along the GOR and there is always something quite out of the ordinary. Torquay for all things surfing, and Anglesea with its extraordinary golf course where kangaroos and golfers share the greens and fairways. 'The kangaroos clearly run the place', was certainly one visitor's impression as she watched golfers shooing kangaroos so they could take another swing. Port **Campbell with its stunning national park, and Warrnambool with nearby Logans Beach where calving of southern right whales takes place.** But to reiterate, pick any town or stretch along the GOR and you won't be disappointed. It is the same with all of its features — its parks, beaches, wildlife, history, people, wine and cuisine, the many activities arising in and about its reaches. Take the eerie landscape of the Petrified Forest near Bridgewater Bay, west of Portland. Here an old grove of moonah trees smothered by sand eventually decayed into petrified trunks.

The Great Ocean Road, while diverse, is easily travelled and has recently been widened and improved with better signage and road markings. That said, its best taken slowly and savoured. Stop en route to appreciate the great hospitality of the locals, wonderful food, wine and good shopping.

Almost every outdoor activity is on offer, from fishing, boating, tennis and golf, to bushwalking, eco-touring, hang-gliding and abseiling. Obviously, there are water sports aplenty, including surfing and scuba diving. Most importantly, appreciate the beauty of this remarkable stretch of coastline that truly deserves its status as an icon of international standing.

plan your trip
make your bookings
create your travel itinerary
www.planbooktravel.com

THE 'GREAT WAR' MEMORIAL

The Great Ocean Road has been called the longest war memorial in the world. Some 3000 returned soldiers from WWI dedicated labour to their comrades who died in that war. The former Diggers used their muscle, sweat and skills to blast the roadway along 100m cliffs and drive it over dense bush-covered mountains.

The men lived in bush camps and the hard, physical work created a high turnover. The work was sometimes dangerous and several men lost their lives. For their labours they initially received ten shillings and sixpence ($1.05) for an eight-hour day. While the work was hard, there was time for fishing, swimming and hunting.

More than 85 years later, travellers along the Great Ocean Road can experience one of the world's most stunning coastal highways characterised by raging surf, huge cliffs, lush forests, scenic beaches and charming resort towns.

The GOR was Howard Hitchcock's vision. Hitchcock came up with the idea of returned soldiers building a coastal strip stretching from Barwon Heads to Warrnambool and proposed that a private trust be used to fund and build it. The first meeting of the Great Ocean Road Trust attracted 500 people to a meeting in Colac on 22 March 1918, where a price tag of £150 000 ($300 000) was proposed to build a road to rival the Corniche in the French Riviera.

Although the inaugural meeting brought in £7000, raising the rest of the money became a challenge almost as daunting as blasting trails through the rugged landscape. Over the years the trust launched numerous appeals and resorted to various schemes such as subdividing and selling blocks of land along the route. A toll operated for 14 years until the Trust handed the road over to the State Government.

Four months after the official launch, construction commenced on the first stretch of road between Cape Patton and Lorne; however, this was abandoned less than a year later after pressure from Lorne residents and settlements to the east. After switching direction, the first section of the road opened in 1922 by Victoria's Governor, Lord Stradbroke, followed by a night of rousing celebration at Erskine House.

Funding shortages and local squabbling caused periodic delays and it would take another decade before the vision of a coastal road from Geelong to Apollo Bay was eventually realised on 26 November 1932. A weekend of festivities greeted the linking of all sections of the road that now ran all the way to Warrnambool. Victoria's Lieutenant-Governor, Sir William Irvine, declared the road officially open at a ceremony near Lorne's Grand Pacific Hotel, the sight where the first survey peg for the road was hammered in 14 years before. A notable absentee was Howard Hitchcock, who had died earlier that year.

On 2 October 1936, the Great Ocean Road Trust handed over the road to the State Government.

THE GREAT OCEAN ROAD MEMORIAL ARCH

GREAT OCEAN ROAD 2–3 DAY ITINERARIES

SURF COAST TO SHIPWRECK COAST
(2-3 Day Itinerary)
Day One: Melbourne to Apollo Bay
Approximate distance: 200km
Approximate driving time: 3hr

Head out of Melbourne over the West Gate Bridge and along the Princes Freeway to Geelong, then on to Torquay, Australia's surfing Mecca. Torquay's famous Surfworld Museum displays the region's fascinating surfing history. With Bells Beach just around the cnr, Torquay is recognised as one of the world's top surfing locations, as well as the beginning of the Great Ocean Road (from the east).

Travel through the coastal townships of Anglesea and Aireys Inlet to Lorne, a resort-style town overflowing with restaurants, cafes and shops that offer a 'civilised' adjunct to the natural beauty of the nearby Angahook-Lorne State Park.

Continue on the Great Ocean Road from Lorne towards Apollo Bay. At this point the contrast between rugged coast and inland forest becomes particularly spectacular. You'll pass a series of tiny hamlets along the way, like Wye River and Skenes Creek, which make worthwhile pit stops for both scenery and local colour.

A slightly less 'ritzy' resort town than Lorne, Apollo Bay retains much of its fishing and farming character and makes a convenient base to explore the waterfalls and rainforests of the Otway National Park.

Day Two: Apollo Bay to Port Fairy
Approximate distance: 200km
Approximate driving time: 2.5hr

From Apollo Bay, the Great Ocean Road takes you through the Otway National Park and farmland along the coast. Stop at Maits Rest for the self-guided rainforest walking trail and experience mountain ash towering over tree ferns and moss-covered undergrowth. Slightly further on from here is a worthwhile side trip to Cape Otway — a 13km winding drive through dense forest replete with wildlife and spectacular coastal views from the headland.

From Lavers Hill onward, the Great Ocean Road outdoes itself for spectacular scenery. It follows limestone cliffs of the Shipwreck Coast — rock formations carved from the mainland over thousands of years and now protected as part of Port Campbell National Park. Highlights include the Twelve Apostles, Loch Ard Gorge and London Bridge. Viewpoints are well signposted with information boards, boardwalks and there is ample parking with easy access.

Just before the fishing village of Port Campbell, the Great Ocean Road threads its way beside fertile wetlands and estuaries, all inhabited by an abundance of birdlife. At Peterborough, there are yet more impressive rock formations within the Bay of Martyrs and Bay of Islands.

Continue on to Warrnambool, a city with a whaling industry heritage that now thrives on whale-watching tourism. If you're here between May and September, keep your eye out for southern right whales off the coast at Logans Beach. Perhaps do some sleuthing in the dunes between Warrnambool and Port Fairy and see if you can unlock the mystery of the fabled Mahogany Ship. Legend has it that a 60 to 200 tonnes Mahogany ship (said to be a familiar site to those who roamed these parts from about 1836 to the 1880s but subsequently covered by shifting sands) is buried beneath the dunes and with it the key to Australia's early exploration. If indeed there is a Mahogany ship, debate rages about how long it has been there and who brought it. Find out what the locals think and join the debate (*see* the Mahogany Ship Mystery p.102–3). Only a short drive on is Port Fairy, a picturesque heritage town and one of Victoria's earliest fishing ports. Many of its limestone and bluestone buildings date from the 1840s and are classified by the National Trust.

Day Three: Return Journey to Melbourne
Approximate distance: 400km
Approximate driving time: 4-5hr

Revisit the coastal route to Melbourne or return by the more direct inland route on the Princes Hwy via Warrnambool, Camperdown, Colac and Geelong.

LORNE BEACH

HERITAGE HIGHLIGHTS
(2-3 Day Itinerary)
**Day One: Melbourne to Apollo Bay
(via the Bellarine Peninsula)**
Approximate distance: 250km
Approximate driving time: 4hr

Head out of Melbourne over the West Gate Bridge and along the Princes Freeway towards Geelong.

Visit Werribee Park Mansion and Point Cook's National Aviation Museum. Both are accessible from the freeway. Slightly further afield near the township of Lara is Serendip Sanctuary, featuring more than 150 species of native birds which can be seen at close range.

Geelong's National Wool Museum is a must see. Housed in a century-old bluestone wool store, it documents the Australian wool industry from fleece to finished garments. Other worthwhile sites include the art deco Eastern Beach Baths Complex and Geelong's vibrant waterfront with its unusual sculptured bollards.

Rather than driving straight on from Geelong to Torquay, take a slight diversion and visit the Bellarine Peninsula's main towns of Point Lonsdale and Queenscliff. Historic Queenscliff mixes elegant 19th-century Victorian architecture with quaint fishermen's cottages, and also features Australia's largest and best-preserved military fort. You'll also appreciate the uninterrupted views of Port Phillip from Point Lonsdale's Rip View Lookout.

From Point Lonsdale it's only a short drive to Torquay where the Surfworld Museum displays the region's fascinating surfing history. With Bells Beach just around the corner, Torquay is recognised as one of the world's top surfing locations, as well as the start of the Great Ocean Road.

The coastline from Torquay to Lorne has been subjected many times to the ravages of bushfires, with the last major fires occurring in 1983, known as the Ash Wednesday fires that claimed 47 lives. Many of the small townships, like Anglesea and Aireys Inlet, have been significantly rebuilt since that time. One prominent survivor of the fires is Aireys Inlet lighthouse, an historic sentinel that can been seen from as far away as Lorne.

Pit stop in Lorne, a resort-style town overflowing with restaurants, cafes and shops that offer a bustling contrast to the natural beauty of the nearby Angahook-Lorne State Park.

Continue on the Great Ocean Road from Lorne towards Apollo Bay. At this point the contrast between rugged coast and inland forest becomes particularly spectacular. You'll pass a series of tiny hamlets along the way, like Wye River and Skenes Creek. These dots on the map were once hubs of the Otways' timber industry and their ensuing tourism potential were key reasons for the Great Ocean Road's establishment.

Beyond Lorne is Apollo Bay, also a resort town but one which retains much of its fishing and farming character. Pop into the information centre in town for comprehensive information on the history of the region.

Day Two: Apollo Bay to Port Fairy
Approximate distance: 200km
Approximate driving time: 3hr

After Apollo Bay the Great Ocean Road threads its way through the Otway National Park towards Lavers Hill. Follow the Shipwreck Coast with its many highlights (see opposite page).

This wild section of the coastline claimed more than 50 ships, many during the goldrush days when immigrants flocked to Victoria to seek their fortune.

The fishing village of Port Campbell marks the start of what was once a lucrative whaling industry that stretched along this part of the coast. Continue on to Warrnambool and visit the city's information centre to learn all about the

WINTER BEACH

heritage of this abandoned industry. Today whale watching has taken over in earnest, and if you're here between May and September, keep your eye out for southern right whales off the coast at Logans Beach.

Only a short drive away is Port Fairy, a picturesque heritage village and one of Victoria's earliest fishing ports. Many of the village's limestone and bluestone buildings date from the 1840s and are classified by the National Trust.

For more fascinating history on southern Victoria's whaling history visit Port Campbell, midway between Apollo Bay and Port Fairy.

Day Three: Return Journey to Melbourne
Approximate distance: 500km
Approximate driving time: 5-6hr

Return to Melbourne via the coastal route you have just experienced, or by the more direct inland route on the Princes Hwy via Warrnambool, Camperdown, Colac and Geelong.

GREAT OCEAN ROAD 3–5 DAY ITINERARIES

NATURE'S BOUNTY
(3-5 Day Itinerary)
Day one: Melbourne to Lorne
Approximate distance: 135km
Approximate driving time: 2hr

Drive from Melbourne along the Freeway to Geelong — gateway to the Bellarine Peninsula and the delights of the Great Ocean Road. Visit the city's picturesque waterfront lined with its humorous hand-painted bollards.

Enjoy the interactive displays, demonstrations and anecdotes of the National Wool Museum, the most comprehensive of its kind in Australia.

Take a detour around the Bellarine Peninsula, one of the most bountiful regions in Victoria and home to wonderful wineries, restaurants and historic homes. Experience the heritage charm of Queenscliff, including the Black Lighthouse.

The Great Ocean Road begins in earnest from Torquay onward, and the road to your first overnight stop in Lorne winds past some of the most spectacular beaches and quaint coastal towns in the state. Turn off the highway just after Torquay to visit the best known surf break in Australia, Bells Beach. Venture inland from either Anglesea or Aireys Inlet to experience the Otway Range hinterland before it transforms into temperate rainforest further down the coast. When you arrive in the coastal resort town of Lorne, stretch your legs on one of the region's many short walks, like Cumberland Falls or Sheoak Falls.

Day two: Lorne to Apollo Bay
Approximate distance: 45km
Approximate driving time: 1hr

Continue along the steepest stretch of the Great Ocean Road to Apollo Bay and spend the day exploring the Otway's rainforest.

Enjoy short walks to several remote waterfalls or a longer walk through beech forests to a secluded lake. Visit the information centre in Apollo Bay for more details.

One of the highlights is the Otway Fly, an elevated walk through the treetops of the rainforest. Overnight in Apollo Bay.

Day three: Apollo Bay to Port Campbell
Approximate distance: 96km
Approximate driving time: 1.5hr

Travel along the most spectacular section of the Great Ocean Road today, where limestone cliffs have been sculpted into a series of gorges, arches, islands and blowholes. Marvel at the Twelve Apostles and learn the amazing survival story associated with the historic wreck of the *Loch Ard*. Stop the car frequently as you travel through the Port Campbell National Park to enjoy myriad clifftop and beach walks. Each feature fascinating geological formations with evocative names like the Bay of Martyrs, London Bridge and the Grotto. Choose from ample accommodation in the nearby fishing village of Port Campbell. A simple pleasure is to idly wander along the banks of the Port Campbell Creek. The creek joins the sea at Port Campbell Bay, an inlet where the waves often howl into the shoreline. One pastime is to watch surfies battle the waves here.

Day four: Port Campbell to Port Fairy
Approximate distance: 85km
Approximate driving time: 1.5hr

Start your day today with a walk at Tower Hill State Game Reserve. At this ancient volcanic crater you can often spot emus, kangaroos, koalas and waterbirds. Continue your drive along the coast to the historic village of Port Fairy. Enjoy fish fresh from the boats in the harbour and take an afternoon walk along the rugged coastline to The Crags. Visit the Port Fairy Visitor Information Centre for details. Accommodation in Port Fairy varies from National Trust-classified fisherman's cottages to luxury bed and breakfasts.

Day five: Return to Melbourne
Approximate distance: 375km
Approximate driving time: 6hr
(via the Great Ocean Road) or
4hr (inland via Colac)

Retrace your steps along the coast or, if you like, take a shorter and more direct route back to Melbourne via Warrnambool, Colac and Geelong.

THE GEELONG BOLLARDS

SPECTACLES ITINERARY
(3-5 Day Itinerary)

Day one: Melbourne to Torquay
Approximate distance: 100km
Approximate driving time: 1.5hr

Set off from Melbourne and make a beeline for the start of the Great Ocean Road. This means enjoying an easy drive down the dual carriageway of the Geelong Rd and through Geelong to Torquay. Whether you're a beach fan or not, the attractions of this surfing Mecca are a great introduction to the atmosphere of the entire coastline.

The mood is best captured in the Surfworld Museum, which details the history of surfing to early Tahitian times.

Check out Torquay's various surfing supermarkets, go for a stroll along the cliff tops, watch the kite surfers on the front beach and survey the surfing action around the headland. Overnight in your choice of accommodation — everything from backpackers to luxury motels.

Day two: Torquay to Aireys Inlet
Approximate distance: 20km
Approximate driving time: 25min

A short drive out of town is Bells Beach, Australia's most famous surf break. Walk along the area's spectacular cliff tops which offer panoramic ocean views and learn about the history and lifestyles of the local Aboriginal tribes on the Koori Culture Walk. Continue on to Anglesea to visit a golf course with more kangaroos than golfers.

The sweeping coastline between Anglesea and Aireys Inlet is made all the more impressive by some remarkable architecture, including one house perched on a pedestal overlooking the ocean.

Take time out from the coastal drive to experience the wildlife bonanza of the hinterland, including wildflower walks and bird-watching extravaganzas at sites like the Coogoorah Wetlands. Overnight in an Aireys Inlet bushland bed and breakfast where you can hand-feed the parrots.

Day four: Aireys Inlet to Warrnambool
Approximate distance: 220km
Approximate driving time: 3.5hr

Today's drive encompasses the most breathtaking scenery of the Great Ocean Road yet. If you stop for brunch in Lorne, then you may choose to head on around the circuitous curves of the road to Apollo Bay.

Much of this section is cut into the cliffs that plunge into the sea far below. The road is overhung with lush rainforest until just after Kennett River (one of the tiny coastal hamlets) where bushland gives way to rolling hills, farms and views to Apollo Bay.

Beyond Apollo Bay, the coast road changes yet again; first the towering trees and tree ferns of the Otway National Park around Lavers Hill, then the dramatic limestone cliffs and windswept landscapes of the Port Campbell National Park.

Known as the Shipwreck Coast, this rugged shoreline boasts the most famous landmarks on the entire Great Ocean Road, and all are right by the roadside, including the Twelve Apostles, Loch Ard Gorge, the Grotto and Sentinel Rock. Such sights are both beautiful and treacherous — more than 1500 ships foundered along here, with only 500 wrecks discovered to date. So there is a lot of discovering still to be done and there are those at work doing exactly that.

Why not stop for afternoon tea in the fishing village of Port Campbell, before heading on to Tower Hill just outside Warrnambool. Here you can climb the top of the hill for great ocean views of the port city and its environs before arriving at your evening's destination. If staying overnight, there is plenty of accommodation to choose from in Warrnambool

PEDESTAL HOUSE NEAR AIREYS INLET

Day five: Warrnambool sightseeing then return to Melbourne
Approximate distance: 345km
(via the Great Ocean Road)
or 265km (inland via Colac)
Approximate driving time: 5.5hr
(via the coast) or 3.5hr (via Colac)

Visit Warrnambool during the winter months and enjoy the amazing sight of southern right whales off Logans Beach. Spend the morning viewing these gentle giants from the custom-built platforms before setting off on your return drive to Melbourne.

Alternatively, discover more about the history of shipwrecks in the area at the Warrnambool Flagstaff Hill Maritime Museum. This life-size village reflects the atmosphere of a coastal port in the 19th century. It includes a bank, printer, sail-maker and ship-builder, pub, church, doctor's office, and an original lighthouse. There is also a glass blower working on the premises.

Return to Melbourne either by the Great Ocean Road or the more direct inland route via Colac.

GEELONG TO TORQUAY

Geelong is a mini metropolis that offers a lively cultural life at the leisurely pace of a big country town. It's worth whizzing down the freeway from Melbourne just to ramble along the city's picturesque waterfront. Here, eye-catching hand-painted bollards line the quay, interspersed with bustling cafes.

Among Geelong's many attractions is the National Wool Museum, the most comprehensive of its kind in Australia. Housed in a renovated wool store, the museum details wool's place in Australian history via a series of displays, demonstrations and anecdotes. Watch shearers at work, experience the conditions they once lived under and learn how to weave a lovely warm woolly jumper.

This is simply the start, because Geelong is the gateway to the Bellarine Peninsula, one of the most bountiful regions in Victoria where you'll encounter world famous wineries, restaurants, spectacular historic homes, and sometimes all three together. Be sure to visit one of these rural jewels, such as Spray Farm, where you can indulge in wonderful local wines and fresh farm food against the glittering backdrop of Port Phillip.

Stride the fairways of international standard links golf courses fringed by ocean beaches, then unwind 19th-century style in one of Queenscliff's heritage hotels. Among the town's historic offerings and located within the grounds of Fort Queenscliff, is the Black Lighthouse. Constructed of Maribyrnong basalt, this is the only original 'black' lighthouse in Australia. Not only is this unusual landmark one of three in the world, it allegedly occupies the site of the first public phone box in Victoria.

From Geelong all roads south seem to lead to the start of the Great Ocean Road at Torquay, Australia's south coast surfing hotspot and nearby Bells Beach, one of the most famous surfing beaches in the world.

HISTORIC GEELONG

GEELONG

www.planbooktravel.com

A BAYWALK BOLLARD

MUST SEE

- Stroll along the Baywalk Bollards and admire the 104 painted wooden sculptures by artist Jan Mitchell. Set around Corio Bay, the sculptures depict characters from Geelong's rich history.
- Visit the art deco seabathing swimming pool and park complex at Eastern Beach, constructed in the 1930s as 'the people's eastside playground'.
- Ride the historic carousel (circa 1882), a restored Armitage-Herschell carousel with a vintage Gavioli band organ
  When: 10.30am–5pm Mon–Fri, 6pm Weekends, 8pm Summer **Where:** on the waterfront beside Steampacket Quay
  Ph: (03) 5224 1547
- Tour the National Wool Museum, located in an historic, bluestone wool store built in 1872, and view the displays of Geelong's, and Australia's, wool heritage
  When: 9.30am–5pm daily
  Where: 26 Moorabool St
  Ph: (03) 5227 0701
  Web: www.geelongaustralia.com.au
- Browse through the Ford Discovery Centre which showcases the 80-year history of the Ford Motor Company in Australia and

Located on the shores of Corio Bay, Geelong is Victoria's second largest city. It has been experiencing a minor tourism renaissance since the 1990s, as a result of initiatives by State Government and local bodies.

Geelong is an industrial, port city with a wool-processing centre and a Ford-engine plant, that once seemed unsuited as a tourist destination. With these industries declining, the city is using its waterfront, recently refurbished, and its manufacturing history as an advantage in the tourist market.

Today, Geelong is an attraction-packed city and the gateway to the Great Ocean Road, Bellarine Peninsula and Surf Coast.

POPULATION
210 000

TORQUAY TO LORNE

Along the weaving stretch of surf-fringed highway between Torquay and Lorne are some of the best-known surf breaks and beaches in Australia — iconic places that help define the country's famous sun, sea and sand reputation for the rest of the world.

Between the scenery of beaches and bushland is a series of equally picturesque villages: Torquay, Anglesea, Aireys Inlet and Lorne. Each has a fascinating history, extending from an enduring connection with local Aboriginal clans to the more immediate history of rapid development since white settlement.

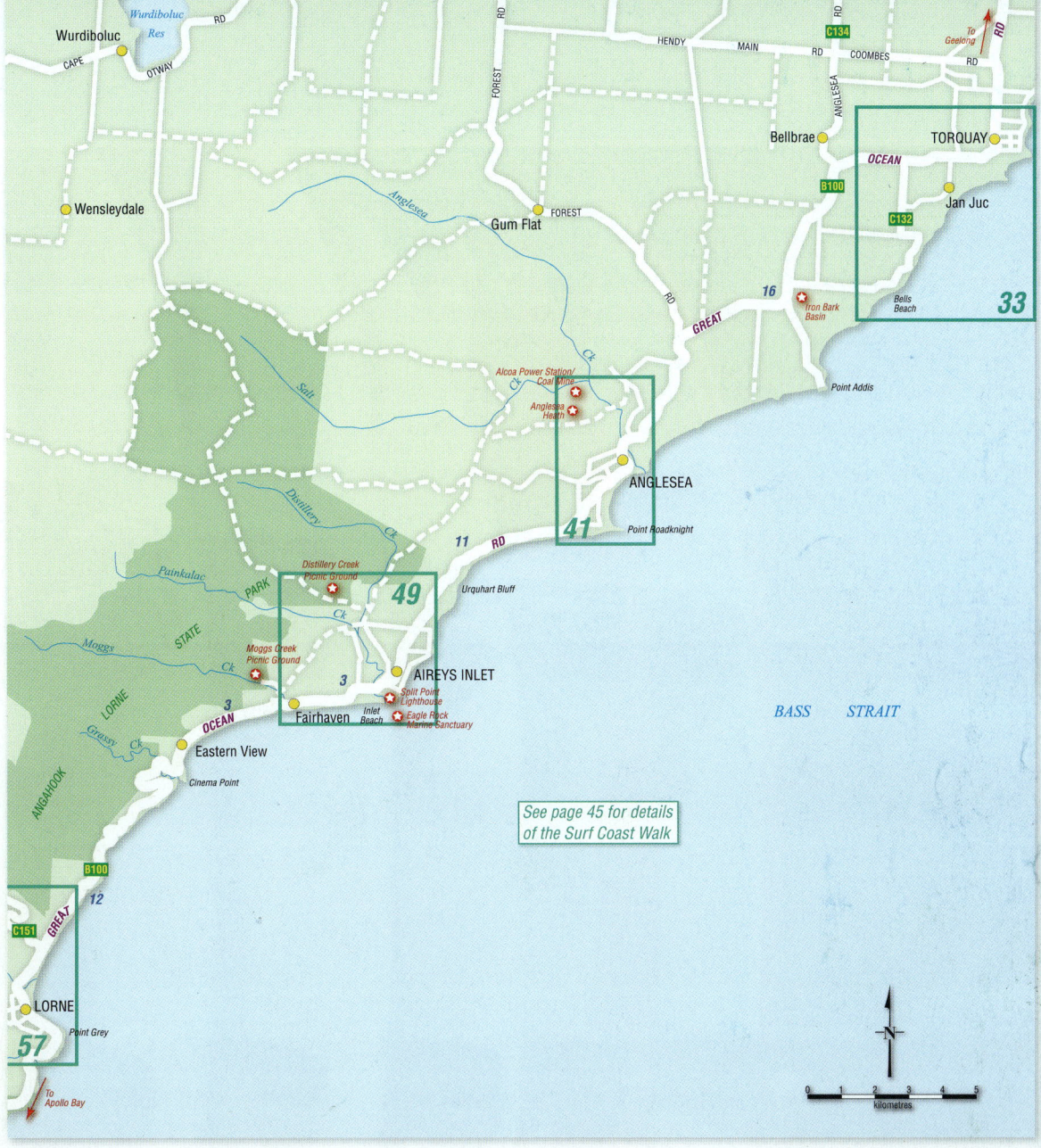

Australia's surfing mecca, Torquay is the place to enjoy every aspect of beach culture, from high-energy water sports to family fun in the sun, not to forget some serious shopping. Two of the world's biggest surf brands were conceived here: Rip Curl and Quicksilver. Each was nurtured by their surf-crazy founders from back-room concerns into the household names they are today. Along the way they also just happened to invent the wetsuit.

On Surf City Plaza surfboards stand in neat rows like soldiers at attention and the 'surf grunge' clothing comes with designer labels and high price tags.

Just beyond Bells Beach is Anglesea, a busy holiday town with an overwhelming array of broad beaches, water-sporting options, and the Otway Range hinterland to explore.

Aireys Inlet is like a sleepy seaside village in comparison with Anglesea, a place defined by its lighthouse that stands sentinel on the rocky red clifftop and can be seen at all times from Lorne.

Lorne, declared an area of 'Natural Beauty and Special Significance' by the Victorian Government, is the quintessential resort town, a coastal playground for the rich and famous with opulent as well as historic homes, and a shopping strip as chic as any in Melbourne. The town is set against the backdrop of the Otway Range and has a restful charm about it. The atmosphere during holiday season is positively electric and well worth a pit stop between more tranquil GOR experiences.

TORQUAY

Torquay is Australia's surfing capital. It is near the world-famous Bells Beach, and the home of major surfing industry companies. Named after the English resort town, it's a popular holiday destination and the official start of the Great Ocean Road. But, if you're not into surfing and surf culture, Torquay may not be for you.

POPULATION
7950

MUST SEE
- Visit Surfworld Museum, the world's largest surfing and beach culture museum.

When: 9am–5pm daily
Where: Surf City Plaza, Beach Rd.

WORTH VISITING
- Figure out the time of day the old-fashioned way at the Sundial on Torquay's Esplanade. A stunning, large circular mosaic made of 12 000 glass tiles, it relates the Aboriginal legend of Mindii. Stand in the centre, and your shadow will show the time of day.

CAN DO
- Visit the Tiger Moth World Adventure Park, which offers mini-golf, a flying fox, a playpark, bikes, volleyball, a maze, a gift shop and coffee shop, regular air shows and canoeing across a lagoon. Scenic Flights are also available, the most popular going over the Twelve Apostles near Port Campbell — the view is superb.
Where: 325 Blackgate Rd, Torquay
Web: www.tigermothworld.com
Ph: (03) 5261 5100
- For an exhilarating experience, try tandem skydiving, for details Great Ocean Road Skydiving **Ph:** (03) 9432 2413
- There is a skate park for the youngsters behind Surfworld Museum in the Surf City Plaza.

NATURAL ATTRACTIONS
- The 1st stage of the 30km Surf Coast Walk begins in Jan Juc and meanders to

TORQUAY

BED AND BREAKFAST IN BELLS BEACH

Bells Beach, taking in stunning coastal views from the clifftops. The walk is in stages, easily joined and left (*see* Surf Coast Walk feature p.44).

WHAT'S ON
Jan: Point Danger 1000m Swim
Apr: Rip Curl Pro Surfing Championship at Bells Beach and nearby breaks during the 10 days of competition.
Web: www.aspworldtour.com
Dec: High Tide Festival

MOVIES
- Family films are screened during peak periods in the theatrette at Surfworld Museum When: from Boxing Day to Australia Day weekend (late Jan), and over Easter.

RETAIL THERAPY
- Visit dozens of surf shops in Torquay, for clothing, wetsuits, boards and surfing paraphernalia. Most stores are in the Surf City Plaza.
- If you wish to purchase non-surf-related items, head to the main shopping area around Gilbert St. There you can purchase food, clothes and giftware.

MARKET TO MARKET
- Cowrie Community Market
  When: from 10am 3rd Sun of the Month Sept–Apr Where: Elephant Walk, Torquay Foreshore (end of Gilbert St).

FOOD & WINE
- Stop off for a beer at the Bells Beach Hotel (also know as the BBH)
  Where: Jan Juc Ph: (03) 5261 5111
- The Rose is located between Torquay and Jan Juc Where: 220 Great Ocean Road
  Ph: (03) 5261 7399
- For fresh and tasty cafe cuisine try Sandbah Cafe When: from 7:30am daily for breakfast and lunch; dinner Fri–Sat Where: 21 Gilbert St.
  Ph: (03) 5261 6414
- For a nice breakfast or lunch, choose one of three cafes/bars on the corner of Baines Cres and Surfcoast Hwy, across from Rip Curl's headquarters.
- For something slightly upmarket Growlers on the Esplanade serves quality modern cuisine.

TEE OFF
- Torquay Golf Club is at the following impressive address: 1 Great Ocean Road.
  Ph: (03) 5261 2005
  Web: www.torquaygolfclub.com.au for a hole-by-hole description.

GO FISH
- Go surf fishing around the creek mouths of Fishermans Beach, at Jan Juc, near Birdrock. Snapper, trevally, whiting, mullet, salmon, bream and flathead could all be among the catch.
- Hook bigger fish, including sharks and barracouta by boat fishing in deep waters.

www.planbooktravel.com

CATCH A WAVE

- According to www.greatoceanrd.org.au, some popular surf beaches around Torquay include:
- Point Impossible: Near Torquay. Beginners/medium.
- Torquay: Beach and point. Beginners/medium.
- Jan Juc area: Beach, Birdrock. Beginners/advanced.
- Bells Beach area: Beaches include Winkipop, Bowl, Rincon, Centreside, Southside. Medium/advanced.

For up-to-date information on all of Australia's major surfing beaches (and much more concerning the world of surfing), see Web: www.coastalwatch.com; for weather forecasts visit the Bureau of Meteorology Web: www.bom.gov.au.

MORE INFO

- Torquay Visitor Information Centre
  When: 9am–5pm daily
  Where: Surfworld Museum, Surf City Plaza, Beach Rd, Torquay
  Ph: (03) 5261 4219,
  @: torquayvic@iprimus.com.au
  Web: www.visitsurfcoast.com

COMING & GOING

- Geelong to Torquay: 24km, 20min
- Torquay to Anglesea: 20km, 16min

SURFING AT BELLS BEACH

SURF'S UP

The Surfworld Museum is a fascinating adventure even if your interest in surfing rates on the mild side. First, there is the most astonishing collection of surfboards, many donated by famous surfers. One board is inscribed with a most hilarious letter from a young boy who had run away to surf. Also grabbing attention is the museum's elaboration of the 'science' of surfing. The museum also houses a wave machine, a paddling machine, an interactive video that teaches you all about waves, and a 'shaper' making a board before your very eyes. It's all very interesting. In addition, there is a gallery of surfing photographs and a movie theatre where you can sit and watch surf movies all day long, if you care to, viewing *Endless Summer* and *Gidget Goes Surfing* and other surfing films. The museum is certainly a lot of fun, with further information accessible at www.surfworld.org.au

GREAT OCEAN ROAD AND GRAMPIANS

35

ROXY STORE TORQUAY
SHOP 5 SURFCOAST PLAZA
TORQUAY VIC 3228 AUSTRALIA
TEL (03) 5261 4768
visit your local roxy store, for the largest selection of roxy gear

ANGLESEA

www.planbooktravel.com

The Great Ocean Road meets the ocean at Anglesea. It has a 'green' focus, being the first town in Victoria to go plastic bag free in all retail outlets. Surrounding Anglesea are many impressive natural environments, including a river, unpolluted beaches, clifftop views of the coast, and a heath full of rare birds and animals.

Anglesea is a bustling holiday town with ample accommodation, eateries and activities of every kind, from horseriding and paddle boating to bushwalking and golf.

POPULATION
2000

MUST SEE
- Play a round of golf among kangaroos. The Anglesea Golf Club is famous for the kangas that are frequently found there. While attempting to feed or pat them is a potentially lethal mistake, they are quite happy to be observed from a reasonable distance (see Tee Off p.42).
- Explore the flora and fauna of the Anglesea Heath. Further information: Parks Victoria Ph: 131 963 Web: www.parkweb.vic.gov.au

WORTH VISITING
- Wander the town's art galleries, including Melaleuca Galleries When: 11am–5:30pm weekends, and daily from the 27 Dec to 30 Jan Ph: (03) 5263 1230 Where: 121 Great Ocean Road Web: www.melaleuca.com.au
- See the operation of the large open-cut coal mine run by Alcoa in the Anglesea Heath Where: Turn onto Camp Rd at the Anglesea Hotel, then turn left into Coalmine Rd — keep an eye out for the lookout on the right-hand side. Tour the mine and Alcoa's nearby power station When: Tues and Thurs,

GREAT OCEAN ROAD AND GRAMPIANS

41

ANGLESEA

SURF SKIING, ANGLESEA

bookings essential.
Ph: (03) 5263 4249
@:angela.daley@alcoa.com.au

CAN DO
- Master the art of surfing at Anglesea beach. Skilled instructors from local surf schools will soon have you upright on a board and looking the picture of professionalism. Remember, age is no impediment to having fun on a surfboard.
- Experienced surfers can head for Bells Beach or Eastern View and Fairhaven along the GOR near the village of Aireys Inlet — the offerings around Anglesea are extensive.
- Windsurf or sail on the protected waters of Point Roadknight.
- Experience Anglesea River on kayak or canoe. Ph: 1300 132 441
  Web: www.gopaddling.com.au
- Learn to surf, Ph: 1300 132 441
  Web: www.gorideawave.com.au

NATURAL ATTRACTIONS
- Explore Anglesea's pristine beaches. First there is the sandy breadth of Anglesea's main beach located just over the dunes from the Anglesea River. Anglesea Surf Life Saving Club members and lifeguards patrol this beach during peak holiday periods (from Christmas to Easter) so it is perfect for families. Further around the bay is the sweeping arc of Point Roadknight Beach, also patrolled and popular with families because the shallow, protected waters are safe for young children.
- Explore the waterways, islands boardwalks, bridges and picnic areas of Coogoorah Park situated on the Anglesea River.
- Pick up the Surf Coast Walk at the half-way mark. This stage goes from Anglesea to Aireys Inlet.

INDIGENOUS CULTURE
- Take the Koori Heritage Walk through the Ironbark Basin (see Breaks and Detours opposite page).

WHAT'S ON
Feb: Rock to Ramp Ocean Swim
Aug: Festival of the One Act Plays
Sept: Angair Wildflower and Art Show

RETAIL THERAPY
- Otway Images Gallery displays and sells fine art photography of the Surf Coast region When: 10:30am–6pm daily
  Where: Shop 1/103 Great Ocean Road
  Ph: (03) 5263 3440
- Acquire locally made art and bric-a-brac from the Surf Coast Art House
  When: 10am–4pm daily
  Where: Cameron Rd

MARKET TO MARKET
- During Easter and Christmas, a market operates on the banks of the Anglesea River.

FOOD & WINE
- Visit Anglesea Hotel for a counter meal and a drink. While you're there, check out the photographs of the pub's long history Where: 1 Murch Cres
  Ph: (03) 5263 1210

TEE OFF
- Anglesea Golf Club is well known for its contented mobs of kangaroos that graze its fairways and greens. There are so many you would almost expect

www.planbooktravel.com

them to be noted as a playing hazard in the course rules. The roos are usually oblivious to the small ball antics going on around them. The club's 18-hole par 73 course is located in a picturesque bush setting just off the GOR. Players rate the course as one of the most challenging (and aesthetically pleasing) on the Surf Coast. The clubhouse has excellent facilities and the bistro serves lunch and dinner daily.

- Anglesea Golf Club
  Where: Golf Links Rd, Anglesea
  Ph: (03) 5263 1582
  @: webmaster@angleseagolfclub.com.au
  Web: www.angleseagolfclub.com.au

GO FISH

- Surf fishing is popular and one can also fish the Anglesea River. Licences are available from the butcher's shop next to Anglesea Post Office.
- Fish for black bream, and other bream from the platforms and piers on the Anglesea River. These can be accessed only on north bank to Bingley Pde. The Anglesea River mouth has whiting, but mainly small snapper.
- Go to Point Roadknight for mullet, flounder, garfish, salmon, snapper, shark and sweep. The ledge here is excellent during low tide on calm days. The boat ramp should be used with care.

BIRDING

- Ironbark Basin contains square-tailed kites and chestnut-rumped heathwrens.

CATCH A WAVE

- Urquhart Bluff, Fairhaven and Eastern View beaches are all considered good surf beaches and are close to Anglesea.

STAYING

- Anglesea Family Holiday Park is a large caravan park that also has many cabins
  Where: Cameron Rd
  Ph: (03) 5263 1583
  Web: www.angleseafcp.com.au
- The Anglesea Hotel offers backpacker accommodation Where: 1 Murch Cres
  Ph: (03) 5263 1210

MORE INFO

- A Visitor Information Kiosk can be found across the street from the public toilets on the Great Ocean Road. Or, call the Torquay Visitor Information Centre
  Ph: (03) 5261 4219
  Web: www.visitsurfcoast.com

COMING & GOING

- Torquay to Anglesea: 20km, 16min
- Anglesea to Aireys Inlet: 11km, 10min

BREAKS & DETOURS

- The long sandy beach at Point Roadknight, about 3km past Anglesea is popular with families. Young children can swim in the calm protected waters, which also benefit windsurfers. The main surf beach is patrolled by surf lifesavers.

GOLFING AT ANGLESEA

SURF COAST WALK

DAIRYING PASTURES MEETS THE OCEAN

There's no better way to take in the diverse scope of the Otways than on foot, and there's no better way on foot than the surf coast walk. Experience natural beauty in abundance, from sweeping panoramas that stretch to the horizon, to the delicate details of fern fronds. Best of all, you don't need to be a seasoned bushwalker to make the most of it. The surf coast walk is constructed as a series of short and readily accessible sections.

Well marked tracks along beaches, cliff lines and in the bush make up a delightful walk from Jan Juc, Anglesea and Aireys Inlet, to Moggs Creek and the Angahook-Lorne State Park. Highlights include Bells Beach, the striking Iron Bark basin, the rugged outcrop of Point Addis and the clifftop vista above Anglesea. It also passes the Anglesea River, Aireys Inlet Lighthouse, Bark Hut and the expansive length of beach along Fairhaven, before entering the wildlife realm of the Angahook-Lorne State Park.

There are numerous access points where you can join or leave the walk. Toilets, drinking water, camping facilities and information boards are located at key intervals along the walk.

STAGE 1: JAN JUC TO BELLS BEACH
4km, 1hr

The closest section of the walk to Melbourne is accessed from the GOR at the western end of the Jan Juc carpark. The track traverses the clifftop through heathland to the 'wave' signpost carpark at Bells Beach, then continues on the coastal side of Bells Beach Rd to steps leading down to the beach.

STAGE 2: BELLS BEACH TO POINT ADDIS
5km, 1.75hr

Access is via either Bones or Jarosite roads from the GOR to the Bells Beach carpark. Follow the access track from the carpark to the beach. This picturesque section of the walk takes in spectacular coastal and bush scenery. From Southside Beach it heads into the Ironbark Basin, passing the ruins of an old jarosite mine and offers stunning sea views through the trees. Emerging from the ironbark forest, the walk continues through heathland along the cliff to a hill climb with great views, before concluding at Point Addis carpark.

STAGE 3: POINT ADDIS TO ANGLESEA
7km, 2hr

Get to the start of this section by taking Point Addis Rd (off the GOR) to the Ironbark Basin carpark. The walk starts at the western end of the carpark and the track descends to the beach. It follows the beach for 1.5km before climbing inland to the clifftops near Eumeralla scout camp outside Anglesea.

STAGE 4: ANGLESEA TO AIREYS INLET (BOUNDARY RD)
10km, 3hr

Pick up the walking track here at the parking spot immediately after the GOR crosses the Anglesea River. This section features Coogoorah Park and views over Anglesea's famous golf course (keep an eye out for grazing kangaroos!) before a steep descent into Hutt Gully, and an equally steep climb up the other side. The track follows Gilbert St to the junction with Boundary Rd. From here you have several choices for the conclusion of your walk.

STAGE 5A: AIREYS INLET (BOUNDARY RD) TO DISTILLERY CREEK PICNIC AREA
2km, 30min

The walk heads to the Distillery Creek picnic area within Angahook-Lorne State

www.planbooktravel.com

Park and from here numerous walks can be accessed within the park.

STAGE 5B: AIREYS INLET (BOUNDARY RD) TO MOGGS CREEK PICNIC AREA
9km, 3hr

This section of the track leads back toward the coast. It takes in Split Point (Aireys Inlet) Lighthouse and passes the graves of two early settlers. The walk can also include a side route to a replica of an early settler's cottage called Bark Hut. It then continues along the beach to Fairhaven where two options are available. Either take Bridge Rd and climb through bushland to an open ridge and heathland for panoramic views from the hilltop (then down again to Moggs Creek picnic area), or continue along the beach towards Eastern View.

WALK SAFETY
- Always stay on the track and keep away from cliff edges
- Always carry plenty of drinking water
- Wear strong shoes or walking boots
- Dress appropriately for the season, and be prepared for the weather to change suddenly
- Take note of track markers and where tracks diverge
- Check tide times before attempting beach sections (yellow emergency markers highlight beach access points)
- Take all rubbish with you
- Consider not using tracks on high fire danger days or during Total Fire Bans
- Fires must only be lit in fireplaces provided, never left unattended and always properly extinguished
- If there is a bushfire, go to the nearest road or campsite, or stay on the beach

MORE INFO
Walk notes and a free Surf Coast Visitor's map are available at Surf Coast Visitor Information Centres located in major centres along the Great Ocean Road.

HIGHLIGHTS BETWEEN ANGLESEA AND AIREYS INLET

TRAVELLING THROUGH FAIRHAVEN

Aireys Inlet, Fairhaven and Eastern View are a series of small communities that overlap at one of the most aesthetically impressive places along the coast. At Fairhaven, just a short drive over Painkalac Creek and its surrounding wetlands, you can see for miles along one of the few 'straight' stretches of the Great Ocean Road. The waves roll in on a long line of sand that continues uninterrupted until the bush-clad hills meet the ocean at Spout Creek.

MUST SEE
- The steep-sided Fairhaven and Eastern View foreshore is dotted with homes overlooking this fabulous view, and many are such impressive architectural creations they are well worth a second glance.
- The GOR continues along the coast almost at sea level, passing beneath a memorial arch at Eastern View which commemorates the efforts of those involved in the GOR's construction. This is a popular visitor stopping point and the history detailed here is a fascinating read.
- From the end of the long Eastern View section the GOR winds inland, quickly reaching heights that enhance the must-stop photo spot at the appropriately named, Cinema Point. There is a small turn-out area here, the last before the road snakes its way back down to sea level for the remaining 15min run into Lorne. It is also at this point the bush of the Otways begins to 'envelop' the GOR, and the eucalyptus from the surrounding gum trees provides an accompanying fragrance.

HISTORICAL INTERESTS
- The current memorial arch at Eastern View is the third to be built on this site, and the fourth over the GOR. The original was at the site of the former tollgate at Cathedral Rock near Lorne, but this was demolished in 1936 when tolls were abolished. A new arch built at Eastern View in 1939 was destroyed by a truck in 1970, and then the Ash Wednesday fires of 1983 reduced the next arch to charcoal. The Ash Wednesday fires also destroyed 177 houses in the area, including almost all the homes in Fairhaven.

NATURAL ATTRACTIONS
- Behind Fairhaven, the rock-garden-like bush of the Angahook-Lorne State Park provides great trails and tracks for walkers, horseriders and cyclists. Many start from Distillery Creek picnic ground near Ironbark Gorge. Like neighbouring Aireys Inlet, Fairhaven is blessed by the splendid colours and sounds of numerous native birds, including honeyeaters, currawongs, king parrots and crimson rosellas.

CAN DO
- The eastern end of the Fairhaven Beach is popular with walkers and fishermen. At the western end of the cove there are good sheltered beginners' waves for surfers. There is also a worthwhile lookout (reached via a walking track) at one of the highest points in the hills of Eastern View near Moggs Creek.

TAKE A WALK WITH THE WILDLIFE:

Opportunities for getting close to native wildlife exist all along the GOR. The Angelsea Golf Club, for example, has several hundred kangaroos sharing the fairways with the golfers. For bird watchers, there are galahs, a variety of rosellas, cockatoos, magpies, wattlebirds, plovers, white-faced herons, willy wagtails, New Holland honeyeaters and even an occasional gang-gang cockatoo. The Angelsea Caravan Park also has an abundance of bird life.

Ocean lookouts dot the GOR. They, too, can be a launching place for exploration. Further on, in Lorne, for example, and along much of the shoreline, there are coastal tidal pools filled with anemones, crustaceans, chitons, sponges, and other invertebrate life. Nearby, cormorants perch on the rocks to rest and dry out their wings.

Rivers hitting the GOR are a good

ECHIDNA BESIDE THE GREAT OCEAN ROAD

GANG-GANG COCKATOO

vantage point for wildlife spotting. Just west of where Cumberland River tumbles into the sea, a colony of bats live in a small cave. Also watch out for black cockatoos here.

Kennett River, in the Angahook-Lorne State Park, has koalas in the gum trees in Grey River Rd. Also watch out for tree creepers (birds), and fantails further up the road in the picnic ground.

Pick any place along the GOR and there are settings for abundant wildlife. At Maits Rest, to choose another random spot, look for what you can see among fern trees, soaring mountain ash trees, and the contorted root systems of myrtle beech trees. Mosses cling to tree trunks. Ferns carpet the forest floor. Sections of the walk cut through a mixture of sclerophyll and temperate rainforest.

Moving on, in the manna gum trees of Otway National Park, there are a great many koalas, although it still requires a sharp eye to spot them.

At the Twelve Apostles, look down from the lookout to spot fairy penguins trundling up the beach at sunset.

On the Great Ocean Road itself, watch out for echidnas. In spite of being well armed against the dangers of the world with a pincushion back of sharp spines, they are vulnerable to cars when crossing the road. For the truly observant, there is a chance of finding a swamp antechinus beside one of the creeks.

All about on the GOR there is a similar banquet of nature and wildlife. At Mt Eccles, you are sure to find koalas, along with cockatoos, kookaburras, Australian shelducks, white-faced herons, little-pied cormorants, Australian grey teals, superb blue wrens, and grey shrike thrushes among others. Possums emerge at dusk, as do eastern grey kangaroos, echidnas, insect bats and owls.

In Portland, look for the Australasian gannet colony off the Portland Aluminium Smelter Nature Walk, but take binoculars, as you can only view them at a distance. At Bridgewater Bay, watch for crested terns; a bit beyond the Petrified Forest, look for Australian fur seals playing in the waves below the cliffs. At Port Fairy, visit Griffiths Island in summer to watch mutton birds.

AIREYS INLET

Aireys Inlet is a small coastal town chiefly consisting of holiday houses, accommodation facilities and a handful of shops. What this town mainly offers its guests is the surrounding natural beauty: pristine beaches, clifftop views, and the nearby Angahook-Lorne State Park.

POPULATION
760

MUST SEE
- Visit the local icon: the Split Point Lighthouse, also known as the 'White Queen' and 'White Lady'. Built in 1891, and fully automated since 1919, the lighthouse is a popular tourist destination. Clifftop views from Split Point are impressive, and there are several signposted walking tracks. While there, visit the Lighthouse Stables Tearoom & Gallery for a snack or to purchase a gift.

WORTH VISITING
- Check out the replica of an 1860s Bark Hut that was burnt down in the Ash Wednesday bushfires in 1983 Where: next to the Allen Noble Sanctuary.
- Hear the Split Point Singers performing every second Wed at St Aidens. Contact Tania Ph: (03) 5289 6526

CAN DO
- Go horseriding. Blazing Saddles offers rides through the Angahook-Lorne State Park, or along the beach. Where: Lot 1, Bimbadeen Dr Fairhaven Ph: (03) 5289 7322, @: blazing@iprimus.com.au
- Great Ocean Road Adventure Tours conducts mountain bike tours through the Otways. They also offer bike and canoe hire Ph: (03) 5289 6841
- Experience a superb two-hour massage that relaxes and releases the flow energy.

Visit Bush to Beach Massage Where: 21 Hartley St Ph: (03) 5289 6538, 0417595840 @: jillo.c@bigpond.com

NATURAL ATTRACTIONS
- Just inside the Angahook-Lorne State Park is the Distillery Creek Picnic Ground, that is accessed from Bambra Rd.
- Explore the rock pools and caves around Inlet Beach, near Painkalac Creek.

WHAT'S ON
June: Winter Solstice Storytelling Festival. Contact Jill Ph: (03) 5289 6538

RETAIL THERAPY
- Art is an important part of Aireys Inlet, particularly the Eagles Nest Fine Art Gallery which presents local artistic talent in a visually arresting space. The gallery itself is architecturally interesting and is something of a local landmark. The artists represented are predominately from the Surfcoast, the Bellarine Peninsula, Geelong and from the Otways. Many of the works are clearly inspired by the land and seascapes of the area where many of the artists both live and work. The reputation of the gallery has grown and there are many repeat visitors. When: 10am–5pm daily during Victorian school holidays, Fri–Mon 1 May–31 Oct, or by appointment Where: 48–50 Great Ocean Rd Ph: (03) 5289 7366

FOOD & WINE
- Try cross-cultural cuisine at John Dawson's Scammells Estate Restaurant Where: 17 Beach Rd (cnr Great Ocean Road), Ph: (03) 5289 6996 @: lmmedia@bigpond.com

AIREYS INLET

- Enjoy a meal in the bistro at the Aireys Inlet Hotel Where: Great Ocean Road Ph: (03) 5289 6270
- Sticky Fingers Honey & T-Room has a certain ring to it and is worth a visit Where: 2–4 Gilbert St Ph: (03) 5289 6645
- Try the tucker at one of the many other cafes on the Great Ocean Road, such as Truffles or Skinny Legs.

GO FISH
- Try to catch some bream, perch or mullet from the estuary of Painkalac Creek.
- See if the salmon, flathead, rock cod, snapper or whiting are biting from the surf.
- Note: fishing is prohibited in the Eagle Rock Marine Sanctuary.

BIRDING
- The Aireys Inlet and Fairhaven region is visited by honeyeaters, currawongs, king parrot reds and crimson rosellas.
- The Allen Noble Sanctuary, between the Great Ocean Road and Split Point Lighthouse, has many native bird species.
- Distillery Creek has a bird hide and also a popular picnic area.

CATCH A WAVE
- Take your board to Eastern View, Fairhaven or Urquhart Bluff.

STAYING
- Aireys Inlet Holiday Park is a caravan park with modern cabins, heated pool, TV lounge and other creature comforts Where: 19-25 Great Ocean Road Ph: (03) 5289 6230 @: info@aicp.com.au Web: www.aicp.com.au
  Ocean Inlet at Fairhaven has three private apartments each with ocean views. Its Coral Cove two bedroom apartment is wheelchair friendly

BREAKS & DETOURS
- Fairhaven beach is a particularly pretty spot, with lifesaver patrols from the end of November through to Easter. Patrols are daily during January, and weekends thereafter.
- Moggs Creek marks the southern end of the Surf Coast Walk. You can often see hang gliders swooping down from the cliffs.
- Eastern View is shadowed by the Memorial Arch, commemorating the

Luxurious Suites with Historic Charm

Waverley House is an historic free-stone residence (circa 1890) which has been carefully and lovingly restored. Exclusive well appointed self contained studio apartments with magnificent old world character and charm. Breakfast provisions supplied daily. Spas available. Ideal central location near beaches, river, shops & restaurants.

Waverley House

Cnr. Great Ocean Road and Waverley Avenue, Lorne
Postal: P.O. Box 60, Lorne 3232 VIC Australia
Ph: (03) 5289 2044
Email: waverleyhouse@iprimus.com.au

www.planbooktravel.com

51

GREAT OCEAN ROAD AND GRAMPIANS

AIREYS INLET NAMESAKE

- WWI veterans who worked on the construction of the Great Ocean Road.
- Angahook-Lorne State Park is accessible from Bambra Rd and Deans Marsh Rd.
- Stop off at Cinema Point for a limited view of Fairhaven and Eastern View beaches from one of the highest viewing spots on the Great Ocean Road.

MORE INFO
- Aireys Inlet Tourism and Traders Association has an informative website Ph: (03) 5289 6230
  @: info@aireysinlet.org.au
  Web: www.aireysinlet.org.au
- Inquire also at the Torquay Visitor Information Centre When: 9am–5pm daily Where: in the Surfworld Museum, Surf City Plaza, Beach Rd
  Ph: (03) 5261 4219
  @: torquayvic@iprimus.com.au
  Web: www.visitsurfcoast.com
- Get information on local wildlife from ANGAIR (Anglesea, Aireys Inlet Society for the Protection of Flora and Fauna), a local community group Where: PO Box 12, Anglesea Ph: (03) 5263 1085
  @: angair@pipeline.com.au
  Web: www.users.pipeline.com.au/angair

COMING & GOING
- Anglesea to Aireys Inlet: 10km, 15min
- Aireys Inlet to Lorne: 21km, 20min

LUNCH AT AIREYS INLET

ANGAHOOK-LORNE STATE PARK

Managed by Parks Victoria, this 22 350ha park has a wealth of flora and fauna, including the tall trees at the ridge of the Otway Range, and many waterfalls, fern gullies, great stretches of coastline, picturesque views and lookouts.

FERNY CREEK NEAR ERSKINE FALLS

The park extends from Anglesea to Cape Patton, and surrounds Aireys Inlet and Lorne. Its many wonders can be explored via approximately 100km of walking tracks.

The varying climate and conditions of the park has led to a great diversity of plants and animals. The major vegetation covering the park's hills and gullies is blue gum, mountain ash, messmate and mountain gum.

Visitors in Spring will encounter blossoming wildflowers. If you head to the northern section of the park around Aireys Inlet, you will find heathlands containing more than 40 varieties of orchids. The park also contains 23 threatened plant species and 18 threatened animal species, including the spotted-tailed quoll. Birdwatchers can find rare hooded plover and rufous bristlebirds.

MUST SEE
- Make sure you check out some of the park's many waterfalls such as Erskine Falls, Straw Falls and Cora Lynn Cascades (*see* Chasing Waterfalls feature p.60). In addition to the Falls Walks, there are many other designated walks, such as the one from Painkalac Dam to the Moggs Creek picnic area, via the fire track.
- Keep an eye open for koalas. Try along the Grey River Rd at Kennett River. Here, the forest lies in a series of saddles with the trees rising to meet the road, so it is possible to catch sight of koalas at eye level.

CAN DO
- You can go horseriding, mountain biking or take a guided bush walk with one of the businesses providing such services.
- Pack a picnic and head to one of the picnic areas at Distillery Creek, Moggs Creek, Blanket Leaf, Sheoak Falls or Grey River.
- Camp next to the Cumberland River about 5km from Lorne. Hike upstream to Cumberland Falls.

STAYING
- There are several overnight camping sites (without facilities), such as on the Cora Lynn Track. There are commercial caravan parks and camping grounds at Aireys Inlet, Anglesea, Lorne, Wye River and Kennett River. Other accommodation is available in adjoining towns.
- You can access the Park via the Great Ocean Rd, Deans Marsh–Lorne Rd, Bambra Rd or Erskine Rd.

MORE INFORMATION:
- Contact Parks Victoria Ph: 131 963, or get park notes online Web: www.parkweb.vic.gov.au/resources/05_0284.pdf
- For horseriding around Aireys Inlet contact Blazing Saddles Where: Lot 1, Bimbadeen Dr Fairhaven Ph: (03) 5289 7322 @: blazing@iprimus.com.au
- For bicycle tours contact Southern Exposure Where: 55B Surf Coast Hwy Torquay Ph: (03) 5261 9170 @: into@southernexposure.com.au Web: http://www.southernexposure.com.au
- Arrange a walking tour through Eco-Logic Where: 3 Camp Rd, Anglesea Ph: (03) 5263 1133 @: ecologic@pipeline.com.au Web: www.ecologic.net.au

LORNE TO APOLLO BAY

While many holidaymakers go no further than Lorne, it is the section of the Great Ocean Road between Lorne and Apollo Bay that is probably the most famous of the entire drive, and certainly the most spectacular.

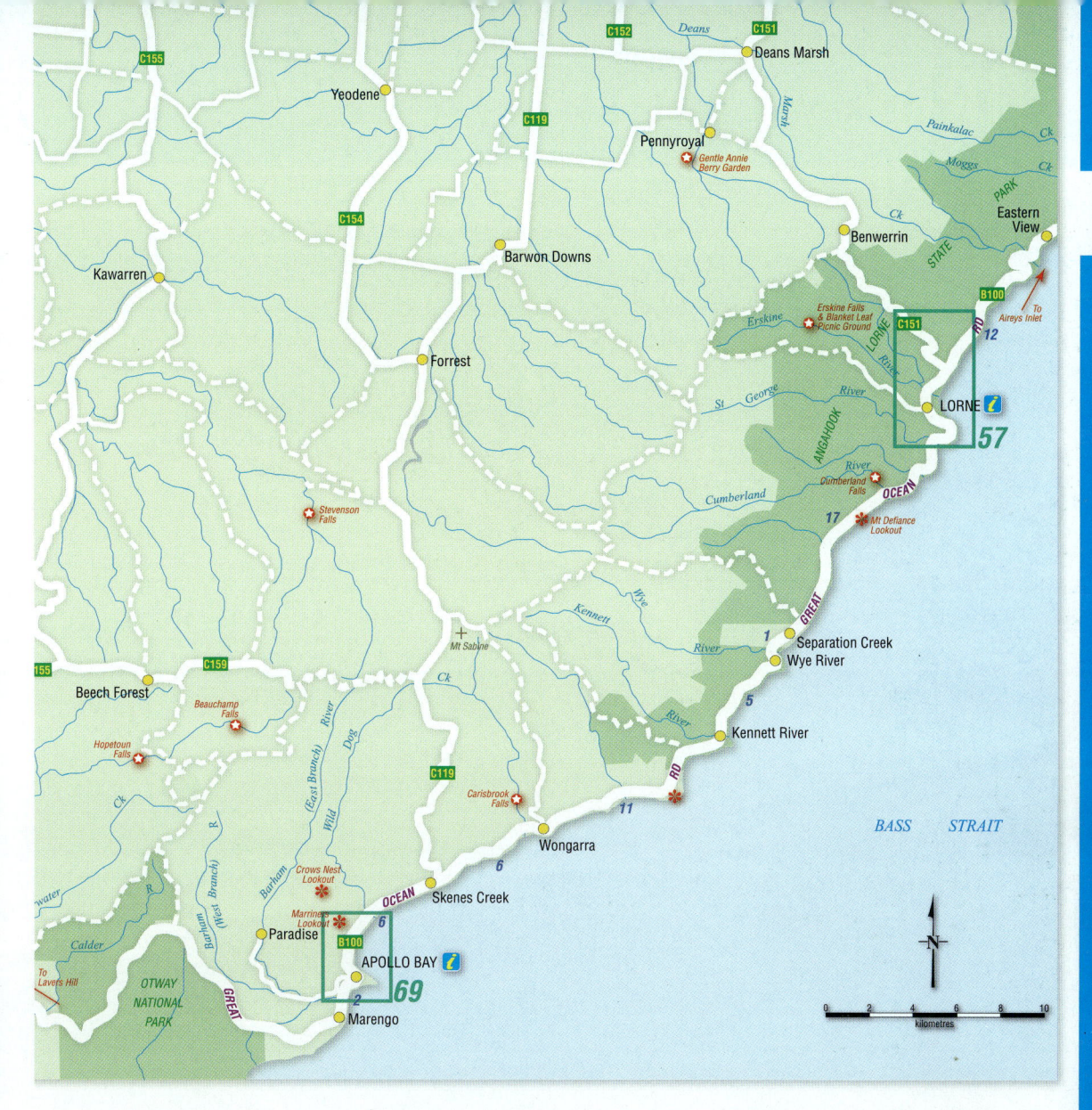

Passing is impossible along this steep and winding section of road which continues almost to Kennett River, so it's best to be happy with a leisurely pace and enjoy the endless tableau of remarkable views.

Savour the experience by stopping frequently at the various turn-outs along the way. A series of striking cliffs not far from Lorne, and immediately inland from the Cumberland River mouth, mark the site of Cumberland River caravan park, which is surely one of the most picturesque settings in Victoria to pitch a tent or park your van.

Just beyond Cumberland River, the GOR shows off some of its most impressive engineering, with the road literally carved and blasted out of the mountainside in many places. Because the road is perched high above the ocean on one side, and overhung with lush Otways vegetation on the other, anything but perfectly calm weather can make the drive feel like a pioneering experience. Expect to have the road either shrouded in sea mist or bathed in brilliant sunshine.

Civilisation reappears in the form of several coastal villages: Wye River, Kennett River and Skenes Creek. The first two are tiny holiday towns, each set amid natural amphitheatres of bushland fronted by postcard-perfect beaches. Steep-sided ranges clad with tree ferns and tall gums add further to the atmosphere of both quiet spots. Wye River is known for its excellent hotel, the Rookery Nook, which overlooks the ocean and Kennett River for its tranquil step-back-in-time seclusion. Not far from Kennett River, the GOR reaches one of its most rewarding lookout points, Cape Patton, giving uninterrupted views over the ocean and grazing land to Apollo Bay in the distance.

From here the road traverses numerous narrow gorges, emerges from the bush into rolling paddocks and passes through rural hamlets like Skenes Creek before reaching Apollo Bay.

LORNE

BEACH NEAR LORNE

Lorne is a famous resort town that overflows with hordes of tourists, mainly from Melbourne, during peak times. This tourist Mecca offers many fine accommodation options.

The main street, Mountjoy Pde, is full of boutique stores and sumptuous eateries, and directly overlooks Lorne's family friendly beach. Erskine Falls, and other natural attractions also entice people to Lorne.

POPULATION

1200

MUST SEE

- Explore spectacular Erskine Falls (see Chasing Waterfalls feature p.60).
- Get your fix of contemporary art at Qdos Arts. The brainchild of Otways-based artist Graeme Wilkie, Qdos features around 90 exhibitions a year. You can also dine at the cafe (see Food & Wine p.59), and accommodation is also available
  When: 9am–6pm Fri–Mon
  Where: Allenvale Rd
  Ph: (03) 5289 1989 to book.

LORNE

LOCAL SHOPS AT LORNE

- Explore Lorne Beach and the grassy foreshore reserve. You will find shower and toilet facilities, picnic tables and barbecues, and a public pool. No dogs allowed on beach between Albert St and Stirling St 1 Dec–30 Apr. Beach is patrolled daily 26 Dec–26 Jan, and weekends and public holidays 24 Nov–31 Mar.

WORTH VISITING
- Hire a paddle boat from the Swing Bridge Cafe Where: on the Erskine River near the bridge as you head into Lorne from Aireys Inlet. Ph: 0408 895 022
- Let the kids (or adults) bounce on trampolines on the foreshore reserve. There is a small cost involved, but it's such fun When: daily during school holidays, and on weekends.
- Visit the Lorne Art Gallery When: 11am–6pm daily, closed Mon Ph: (03) 5289 1288 Where: upstairs, Level 1/1 William St (next to the Blue Lounge)
- Lorne has two pubs: the Lorne Hotel and the trendy Grand Pacific Hotel. Both are on Mountjoy Pde.

CAN DO
- Play a round of mini-golf at Shooters Where: Erskine Falls Rd Ph: (03) 5289 2666

NATURAL ATTRACTIONS
- Go see Erskine Falls and other local waterfalls (see Chasing Waterfalls feature p 60).
- Gain a bird's-eye view of Lorne's Loutit Bay and the Great Ocean Road from Teddys Lookout.
- Explore the rock pools around Lorne's foreshore, or go snorkelling — both can also be done as part of a tour with Eco-Logic Ph: (03) 5263 3133 @: ecologic@pipeline.com.au Web: www.ecologic.net.au

HISTORICAL ATTRACTIONS
- View the photographic exhibition on Lorne's history When: 1pm–4pm first Sun of every month, thanks to the Lorne Historical Society Where: 1 Clissold St Ph: (03) 5243 1249, 0417 517 253
- Lorne's historic buildings include the Grand Pacific Hotel, Erskine House, the pier, several churches and the swing bridge.

WHAT'S ON
Jan: Pier to Pub, Mountain to Surf Run
Apr: Pioneer Festival at Deans Marsh
Dec: Falls Music Festival
Web www.fallsfestival.com

MOVIES
- Lorne Theatre shows films year-round in pleasant old-style surroundings Where: Mountjoy Pde, near the corner of Grove Rd Ph: (03) 5289 1272

RETAIL THERAPY
- Stroll down Mountjoy Pde to find a great assortment of stores (see Shopping and Eating Your Way Through Lorne opposite page).
- Buy fresh seafood, including crayfish, from the pier.

www.planbooktravel.com

SHOPPING AND EATING YOUR WAY THROUGH LORNE

Lorne seems to have two main types of clientele. Firstly, there are young people who flock in their thousands to Lorne for the Falls Music Festival, or for the 'schoolies week' rampage that marks the end of Year 12 studies. Secondly, and more importantly, Lorne caters for couples and families who have the financial resources to enjoy the splendour of an unmarket resort town.

One major way visitors ritually part with their cash in Lorne is at the shops along Mountjoy Pde. There, visitors will find clothes, giftware, books and many other items. This shopping strip has a major advantage over suburban malls: its location gives great views of the beach.

Another major way Lorne tempts its visitors is at its fine restaurants. Mountjoy Pde has one of the best selections of eateries you could find in such a small area, at least anywhere in Australia.

'The Arab' has changed significantly since its heyday in the 1960s. However, it still serves quality Middle Eastern cuisine. Other top-class restaurants include Rief's, Tirami-Su (Italian) and Kostas (Greek).

For families travelling on a tight budget, Lorne is probably not the ideal destination for a long stay; it can be quite pricey. But, if you fancy luxury with a touch of indulgence to go with your experience of natural wonders, then Lorne is perfect.

MARKET TO MARKET

- The foreshore reserve is home to occasional markets. Pick up a copy of *What's On* from the Lorne Visitor Information Centre for details.

FOOD & WINE

- Go to the funky Kafe Kaos for a meal, especially breakfast.
- Visit Lorne's venerable The Arab Restaurant, which specialises in Middle Eastern food, though you can also get a pasta and a latte.
- Try the excellent modern cuisine and extensive wine list at Rief's.
- Go Italian in the unlikely named restaurant, Tirami-Su.
  Where: 1A Grove Rd (just around the corner from Mountjoy Pde)
  Ph: (03) 5289 1004

GREAT OCEAN ROAD AND GRAMPIANS

The township of Lorne is the premier tourist destination of the Great Ocean Road, and the premier venue in Lorne is the Lorne Hotel. The hotel offers guests the very best in hotel accommodation, meals, bar and live entertainment facilities. Visiting the Lorne Hotel is sure to leave a lasting impression with its breathtaking views, superb hospitality and entertainment.

Lorne Hotel

Mountjoy Pde
Lorne, Victoria 3232
Ph: 5289 1409 fax: 5289 2200
info@lornehotel.com.au
www.lornehotel.com.au

LORNE

BEAUCHAMP FALLS

CHASING WATERFALLS
There are many waterfalls near Lorne. Erskine Falls is probably the most famous, and it is truly spectacular. To get there, you drive up Erskine Falls Rd, and turn off at the signpost. After a few kilometres downhill is the carpark. From here walk down the usually misty path to the lookout. You can also explore the paths and rocks under the falls. It is worth bringing a picnic and stopping off at the Blanket Leaf picnic ground. You may want to visit other falls in the area, including Beauchamp, Sheoak, Henderson, Phantom, Kalimna, Cumberland, and the Cora Lynn Cascades.

- Qdos Cafe (formerly ArtzBar), in the Qdos Arts complex When: 9am–6pm, closed Wed Where: Allenvale Rd
Ph: (03) 5289 1989
Web: www.qdosarts.com

TEE OFF
- Lorne Country Club is a nine-hole course, played as an 18-hole course. Views of the sea and bushland add to the experience. The licensed bar also serves meals
Where: Holliday Rd Ph: (03) 5289 1267

GO FISH
- Lorne Pier is a popular site for fishing.
- When the weather is calm, boat fishing around the many close inshore reefs can yield snapper, salmon, trevally, barracouta, whiting, garfish, sweep, pike and gummy shark.
- There are numerous rock ledges for surf fishing — be careful.
- The Erskine and St George rivers contain highly sought after trout, with the estuarine sections offering bream.
- Fishing Licences, which are required for anyone 18 years and over, are available from the Lorne Foreshore Office opposite the supermarket, the Lorne Newsagency, Riordans Hardware and BP Service Station.

CATCH A WAVE
- Lorne beach is good for beginners and surfers with medium proficiency, rather than those who are after a big challenge.

STAYING
- Erskine House, now part of the Mantra Erskine Beach Resort, is the oldest permanently operating guesthouse in Victoria.
Ph: (03) 5289 1209
@: res@erskineonthebeach.com
Web: www.erskineonthebeach.com
- The Cumberland Lorne Resort is another institution. Controversially renovated a few years ago, this luxury establishment offers guests a range of recreational facilities, including pool, sauna and tennis courts.
Where: 150 Mountjoy Pde
Ph: (03) 5289 2400
@: reservations@cumberland.com.au
Web: www.cumberland.com.au
- The trendy Grand Pacific Hotel is another Lorne landmark.
Where: 268 Mountjoy Pde
Ph: (03) 5289 1609
@: grandpacific@ozemail.com.au
Web: www.grandpacific.com.au

KENNETT RIVER NEAR LORNE

www.planbooktravel.com

Mantra Erskine Beach Resort offers something for all tastes, from restaurants and bars, sauna and Day Spa (opening June 2006), to an enclosed climatic heated lap pool, gymnasium, tennis and volleyball courts, croquet and lawn bowls.

Featuring a selection of stylishly appointed rooms, Mantra Erskine Beach Resort offers a range of accommodation from hotel rooms to resort suites. The one and two bedroom apartments are fully self-contained and feature kitchen and laundry facilities, separate lounge and dining areas, reverse cycle air conditioning, private balcony, TV and DVD player. All rooms feature ocean or garden views, and some offer spa baths.

At Mantra Erskine Beach Resort it's all about choice. We give you a menu of services and facilities and you decide how to enhance your stay.

Mantra Erskine Beach Resort

Mantra Erskine Beach Resort
Mountjoy Parade, Lorne, Victoria 3232
PH: (03) 5289 1209
Fax: (03) 5289 1185
erskine.res@mantraresorts.com.au
www.erskinebeachresort.com.au

mantra
erskine beach resort

LORNE

MORE INFO
- Visitor information centre
  When: 9am–5pm daily Where: 144 Mountjoy Pde, Ph: (03) 5289 1152
  @: lornevic@iprimus.com.au
  Web: www.visitsurfcoast.com/lorne
- Also check out www.lornelink.com.au

COMING & GOING
- Aireys Inlet to Lorne: 21km, 20min
- Lorne to Apollo Bay: 45km, 50min

DAY TRIPS
- Conveniently situated between Lorne and Apollo Bay, Wye River is one of the Great Ocean Road's most popular seaside camping spots. Campers have been pitching their tents at Wye River for generations, lured by the unspoiled sea, surf and forests, and making Wye River their own piece of paradise. Add fishing, abundant wildlife, numerous nature walks, fresh air and the free-flowing river to the equation and you have the perfect destination for a holiday or bracing day out. An essential part of Wye River's charm is that there are few distractions from the area's natural attractions. Just a pub, a general store, camping grounds, caravan parks and a few B&Bs.
- Take a walk from Wye River to Separation Creek. It's a 30min walk along Paddy's Path which follows the old tramway route that connected the first timber mill to the jetty at Point Stuart. Now an inland bush path with lush vegetation and great views of Wye Bay.
- Stroll along the river banks. The Kennett River walk starts at the bridge and goes through the wetlands (about 40min). The Wye River walk starts at the playground next to the store and winds along the river (about 30min).
- Follow the beach walks north or south either from Wye River to Kennett River or Wye River to Separation Creek. Whichever way you choose takes you to clear rock pools where starfish, crabs and other sea creatures abound.
- Visitor information centres have maps and details about longer inland walks.
- While walking, watch the birds, as they are many and varied, among them king parrots, gang-gangs, rosellas, currawongs, wattle birds, robins and finches, as well as rare ruffos, kookaburras and sacred king fishers.
- Check out the wildlife, including bats, echidnas, wallabies, possums, whales (in winter) dolphins and seals — all are on view for those with patience and a keen eye; koalas inhabit the Grey River Rd at Kennett River.
- Take a picnic as there are plenty of picnic

LIGHTHOUSE NEAR LORNE

www.planbooktravel.com

sites here, all with super views, or you can simply spread a blanket where you fancy; but remember to clean up.
- Lookouts at Mt Defiance and Cape Patton offer superb views of the rugged coastline and, at Cape Patton the rolling hills behind Apollo Bay.
- Eat at the Rookery Nook at Wye River for old-style hospitality Ph: (03) 5289 0240
- Visit Scully Mill Farm offering free-range eggs, firewood, farmstays and an art gallery Ph: (03) 5289 0462
- Take a scenic drive. Many of the roads from the Great Ocean Road join at the top of the Otway Range on the unmade Benwerrin–Mt Sabine Rds. This allows for circular drives to see the forests, waterfalls, lakes and hamlets of the hinterland. Maps essential and may be obtained from local general stores and information centres.

BREAKS & DETOURS

- Angahook-Lorne State Park on your left and the ocean on your right makes this one spectacular stretch of Hwy (*see* Angahook-Lorne State Park p.52)
  Ph: 131 963
  Web: www.parkweb.vic.gov.au
- Check out the ocean views from lookouts at Mt Defiance and Cape Patton.
- Stop and explore the Cumberland River estuary. Take the track inland to Cumberland Falls.
- Detour to Beauchamp Falls (20km), where there's a picnic area and a walk to the falls.
- Take a cooling dip at Wye River, Kennett River or Skenes Creek (*see* Day Trip p.62).

FALLS WALKS

- Erskine Falls Lookout (easy/moderate)
  Starting at the Erskine Falls carpark, walk 150m to first lookout (15min return); 350m to lower lookout (30min return).
- Sheoak Falls (moderate)
  This 3km, 40min return walk starts at the Sheoak Falls carpark, off the GOR (watch for signposts), about 3km past Lorne towards Apollo Bay. There are great views of the rocky coastline. Head inland through a steep-sided valley to the base of Sheoak Falls, then there is the option of continuing on past Swallow Cave.
- Sheoak–The Canyon–Phantom Falls (strenuous)
  Starting from the Sheoak picnic area, this walk winds between the 8m walls of The Canyon, and takes in both Won Wondah Falls and Henderson Falls, before continuing along Henderson Track to Phantom Falls, and then along the St George River to the Allenvale carpark. Head back to the Sheoak picnic area along the road (8.6km, taking about 4.5hr return).
- Cumberland Falls (strenuous)
  Starts at the Cumberland River Reserve, which can be reached by turning off the GOR about 5km out of Lorne towards Apollo Bay. Follow the track to the Falls; it goes for 6km, and takes about 3.5hr return
- Erskine Falls–Lorne (strenuous)
  Check with Visitor Information before attempting this walk — it is no-go if water levels are high. You should also organise a lift so that you don't have to make the return trip — it is 7.5km and 3hr one-way. The walk begins at the Erskine Falls carpark and includes Straw and Splitter's falls and a natural amphitheatre used in the 19th century for church services. It continues to the bridge over the Erskine River in Lorne.

- Take a detour up Kennett River's Grey River Rd for some koala spotting.
- Head inland to Deans Marsh and the surrounding rural communities. You can pick berries in the Pennyroyal Valley in summer.

GREAT OCEAN ROAD AND GRAMPIANS

The 4½ star fully refurbished Cumberland Lorne Resort offers one and two bedroom apartments, all with private spa and balcony. Resort facilities include indoor heated swimming pool, Aqua Restaurant and Bar, Kids Club, spa and sauna, tennis and squash courts.

Cumberland Lorne Resort

150 Mountjoy Parade, Lorne
Ph: (03) 5289 2400 Fax: (03) 5289 2256
Freecall: 1800 (03)7 010
reservations@cumberland.com.au
www.cumberland.com.au

cumberland lorne resort

HIGHLIGHTS BETWEEN LORNE AND APOLLO BAY

WORTH VISITING

- Located 7km south of Lorne on the GOR (heading towards Wye River), the Cumberland River Holiday Park has cabins and camping facilities set in a peaceful and picturesque valley lined with majestic cliffs. Walk to swimming beach, surf and estuary fishing. An excellent base for the nearby walking tracks and waterfalls, including Cumberland Falls (a 6km, 2.5hr return walk along Cumberland River).
- Look back at Cumberland River and the coast from the spectacular Castle Rock and Langdale Pike lookouts. Explore Jebbs Pools only a short way up the river gorge. Other walks from here take you to Sheoak River, Kalimna Falls and Erskine Falls.
- Wye River may be small but this holiday town 161km from Melbourne on the GOR between Lorne and Apollo Bay caters for a remarkable number of people during summer, so choose your time to visit. Facilities include a great pub, the Rookery Nook (which also has accommodation), a post office and general store (which sells petrol) and a surf club. There are free electric barbecues next to the general store and on the foreshore. Most houses are holiday homes, many of which are available for rent.
- Kennett River is a tiny holiday hamlet about 167km south-west of Melbourne. At first glance, it looks like just another beautiful bush and beach cove with a creek meandering through the middle, but there are quite a number of holiday homes secreted among the trees. Facilities include a small general store adjacent to the caravan park (a picturesque location in itself) and a few new picnic tables down by the river. The town was originally called 'The Kennet' after an English river and apparently the second 't' was added mistakenly by the Roads Board when they upgraded the bridge in the 1960s. Many locals, including the owners of the caravan park, insist on using the original spelling.
- A highlight near Kennett River is the lookout at Cape Patton, which has breathtaking views, day and night, along the rocky coastline, out to sea, and across to the Otway Range towards Apollo Bay in the west.
- Skenes Creek is a small farming and holiday community 6km east of Apollo Bay. From here, an alternative route to Geelong (and Melbourne) runs inland through the Otway Range. The wide and sandy Skenes Creek beach is one of the best on the coast for swimming and fishing, and can present good surfable waves in the right conditions. Skenes Creek Rd and the dramatic Wild Dog Rd undulate ever-upward into the heart of the lush Otway forests. At the top of Wild Dog Rd is Turtons Track. This winds beneath mountain ash, tree fern forests and mossy valleys, and is often made more ambient by veils of mist.

CAN DO

- Swimming, surfing and bushwalking are fantastic at Wye River. Walking tracks around Wye River and Separation Creek take in all the quiet bush beauty and beach walks pass rock pools that teem with marine life.
- Bushwalks to waterfalls, drives through the Otway Range, boating, fishing, swimming and surfing.
- At Skenes Creek, one of the best ways to experience magical routes like Wild Dog Rd is on horseback, and it just so happens that a trail ride company operates right here: Wild Dog Trails.
Where: Wild Dog Rd, Skenes Creek
Ph: (03) 5237 6441

NATURAL ATTRACTIONS

- Birdwatchers, keep an eye out for gang gangs, cockatoos, king parrots, crimson rosellas, currawongs, and bower birds. The best time to spot four-legged wildlife is in the evening. Echidnas, koalas, kangaroos and possums are a common sight. Out to sea, you may be lucky enough to spot whales in the colder months and dolphins in the warmer months.
- Native fauna isn't shy around Kennett River. It is a great place to spy kangaroos, native birds and especially koalas. Grey River Rd which runs out of Kennett River, and the Grey River Reserve further inland, are good koala spotting and picnic sites.
- At Skenes Creek, parrots in myriad colours are common and platypuses are sometimes seen upstream in the creek.

HISTORICAL INTERESTS

- Early road surveyors noted that the section between Cape Patton and Lorne (which includes Kennett River and Wye River) was the most difficult part of the GOR to construct. Rock falls and road closures between Cape Patton (just west of Kennett River) required cliff faces to be stabilised with concrete and anchored cables.
- Like Wye River, Kennett River was already a popular fishing and camping resort in 1919 before the GOR between Apollo Bay and Lorne was completed.
- Aboriginal shellfish middens, some as old as 15 000 years, can be found at many of the freshwater outlets along this section of the coast.
- The Katabanut, or King Parrot people, inhabited the area for thousands of years before white settlement in the 19th century. By the late 1880s Wye River was a small farm and fishing camp accessed by a rough 2m-wide track which ran 37km across the Otway Range to Forrest. Tourists and fishermen began visiting the area at the turn of the century when the first

www.planbooktravel.com

jetty was built. An attempt at timber milling was made around the same time (by the Bluegum Timber and Transport Company) and Wye River's population grew briefly to 150 before the mill was abandoned in 1919.

GO FISH

- Mullet and bream bite near the river mouth, and salmon, trevally and whiting are caught off rock points both sides of town. On the point at Wye River there is a kelp forest — an amazing species of kelp that grows up to 7m long. There is a small boat ramp between Wye River and Kennett River. Remains of the 1899 and 1910 piers are still visible closer to town.

RETAIL THERAPY

- Although there are no shops at Skenes Creek, many of the small farms and converted buildings in the forest are given over to arts, crafts and a variety of organic produce.

STAYING

- Facilities include a protected camping ground on the foreshore (just left of the creek mouth) and a range of guesthouse and B&B options.

FOOD & WINE

- About 2km along Skenes Creek Rd above the town is Chris's Beacon Point Restaurant, fine dining of international standard, and coastal views to match. Chris Talihmanidis is a well-known restaurant identity of 30 years standing in the area. Talihmanidis also runs the Seagrape Wine Bar & Grill in Apollo Bay When: daily for lunch and dinner Where: Skenes Creek Rd, Skenes Creek Ph: (03) 5237 6411
- Also worth the 15min drive is the well-stocked Tanybryn Tea House and Gallery, a craft shop and cafe with beautiful views.
When: 10am–5pm Thurs–Mon, closed July to mid-Sept
Where: cnr Skenes Creek and Wild Dog Rds
Ph: (03) 5237 6271

MORE INFO

- The Kennett River Caravan Park provides information about the region for visitors. There is plenty of accommodation available at both the caravan park and local B&Bs.
Ph: (03) 5289 0272
Web: kennettriver.com

65

GREAT OCEAN ROAD AND GRAMPIANS

Tranquil Bushland Setting with Ocean Views

Early Australian — style, self contained cottages situated beside the Erskine River in a delightful, sloping peaceful bushland setting. Near beaches, bushwalking, shops & restaurants, each cottage has a unique view over Lorne and the surrounding tree covered hills.

Great Ocean Road Cottages

10 Erskine Ave
Lorne, Victoria 3232
Ph: (03) 5289 1070 Fax: 5289 2508
Email: greatoceanrdcotts@iprimus.com.au
Website: www.greatoceanroadcottages.com

APOLLO BAY TO PORT CAMPBELL

After leaving Apollo Bay you enter a different realm, a section of the Great Ocean Road replete with shipwreck relics and tales of sea rescue against imposing backdrops of rugged cliffs and rocky sentinels. This describes the experience of the Twelve Apostles Marine National Park, but before this the road heads inland near its southernmost point, through some of the most spectacular bushland in Victoria, the Otway National Park, where pristine natural beauty and fascinating heritage intertwine.

This ocean-swept length of the GOR features some evocative coastal towns. Emerging into farmland again, the road winds west past Hordern Vale, Glenaire and Johanna, small settlements nestled in fertile river valleys. Each is home to dairy cattle and grazing sheep, and their proximity to myriad attractions make them popular places to stay.

After all, the remarkable sights and stories of the Shipwreck Coast and the area around Port Campbell are why many people drive all this way. 'I have seldom seen a more fearful section of coastline,' explorer Matthew Flinders wrote in the early 1800s as his ship rounded Cape Otway. His observation turned out to be dire for many ships and sailors that followed. The sea floor along this 130km length of coast is littered with countless wrecks, prey to a brutal shore and wild weather.

Be awed by the size of the natural formations, from sheer cliffs and gorges to the famous family of monoliths that is the Twelve Apostles. The coast is at its most impressive when being pummelled by huge Southern Ocean swells and howling winds. Blowholes blast skyward and the sea swirls around the outcrops and cliffs like a boiling cauldron.

See Pudding Basin Rock, Island Arch, the Razorback, Mutton Bird Island, Thunder Cave, the Blowhole, Baker's Oven, London Bridge and the Grotto — evocative names for amazing phenomena. The Twelve Apostles (only eight are left standing) are an experience all of their own. These mighty giants are internationally famous icons of the GOR and a central feature of the national park. The tallest is about 45m, while the limestone cliffs from where they can be viewed are even higher, many up to 70m.

All the natural wonders along this 27km stretch are protected within the 1750ha Port Campbell National Park. This narrow coastal strip extends from Princetown to Peterborough with the small township of Port Campbell right at its heart.

GOLF AT APOLLO BAY

APOLLO BAY

www.planbooktravel.com

Once a sleepy coastal fishing village, Apollo Bay has experienced a tourist boom during the past decade. It is a measure of the popularity of the Great Ocean Road that land values have soared and the main street now abounds with cafes and shops. Still, Apollo Bay retains much of its original charm as a resort village built around the sweeping arc of the harbour, set against the lush, green foothills of the Otway Range. The irresistible lure of beach and rainforest guarantees a variety of attractions and activities from surfing and fishing to nature walks in the forests, sightseeing or simply relaxing all in a place of beauty and serenity.

POPULATION
3000

MUST SEE

- Explore the Otway Range. Apollo Bay is situated at the foot of the Otways and is the ideal place from which to explore this diverse hinterland of rainforests, waterfalls, flora and fauna (see The Otways p. 74).
- Laze on Apollo Bay Beach. A wide sandy beach, fringed by a grassy reserve, with protected waters that make it a safe and popular beach for families.
- See the seals on Henty Reef, part of the Marengo Reefs Marine Sanctuary. Boat tours available at Apollo Bay Fishing and Adventure Tours. Ph: (03) 5237 7888
- Tour Cape Otway Lightstation precinct and climb to the top of the lighthouse for magnificent panoramic views. Built in 1848, the lighthouse is one of Australia's oldest and the lighthouse keepers' quarters are the oldest and largest in the country. Guided and self-guided tours daily
  Where: Lighthouse Rd, Cape Otway, off the Great Ocean Road, west of Apollo Bay Ph: (03) 5237 9240
- The Otways is famous for glow-worms, which are actually the larvae of fly-like insects called fungus gnats. During holiday periods you can see them on guided night walks, but please don't touch the glow-worms or shine lights on them.

WORTH VISITING

- Enjoy the spectacular views of Apollo Bay and the Great Ocean Road at Marriners Lookout.
- Take an afternoon or evening tour and watch how the dark rainforest gullies of the Otways twinkle to the soft light of glow-worms at Melba Gully State Park.
  Ph: (03) 5237 6080
- See the foreshore sculptures. Nine artists have crafted sculptures — all in beautiful local timbers — ranging from fountains to seats, seals, a seahorse and decorative poles.

APOLLO BAY

APOLLO BAY

seafood and other gourmet dishes. Dine on a hillside with ocean views. Chris's also has villas where you can sleep off the night out Where: 280 Skenes Creek Rd Ph: (03) 5237 6411
- Go for the pasta at The Spaghetti Restaurant Where: 1 Moore St Ph: (03) 5237 6551
- Eat at Nautigals because we love the name and the Asian-inspired food is recommended Where: 58 Great Ocean Road Ph: 0402 825 590.
- Try the Bay Leaf Gourmet Deli for innovative and delicious food in a friendly, casual atmosphere Where: 131 Great Ocean Road Ph: (03) 5237 6470

TEE OFF
- Play a round of golf at picturesque Point Bunbury, a 9-hole course (played as an 18-hole) overlooking the ocean and bay Ph: (03) 5237 6474

GO FISH
- The ocean and rivers around Apollo Bay abound with fish for commercial and recreational fishing. You can fish from the jetty, various spots along the coast or the inland rivers of the Otways, like the Barham River where trout are plentiful.
- Hire a boat or take a fishing tour where they'll teach you the correct method of reeling in a big one Ph: (03) 5237 7888
- Eighteen-year-olds and over must have a fishing licence, which can be purchased at Apollo Bay Sports Store, Apollo Bay Surf and Fish and Sportscene, Colac.

CATCH A WAVE
- The protected waters of Apollo Bay are popular with families and ideal for swimming. Serious surfers will find more suitable waves nearby.

STAYING
- Reef View Apartments offer, luxury with an ocean view. Three-bedroom apartments, heated swimming pool, spas and sauna Where: cnr Great Ocean Road and Ocean Park Dr Ph: 0419 533 681 Web: reefview.tourvic.com.au
- Marriners Lookout B&B, stay on hilltop farm flanked by rainforests overlooking the ocean Where: 155 Marriners Lookout Rd Ph: (03) 5237 6450
- Great Ocean View Motel has rooms with views Where: 1 Great Ocean Road, Ph: (03) 5237 6527
- Apollo Bay has a wide range of accommodation, including backpacker. For more information: Web: www.greatoceanview.com.au

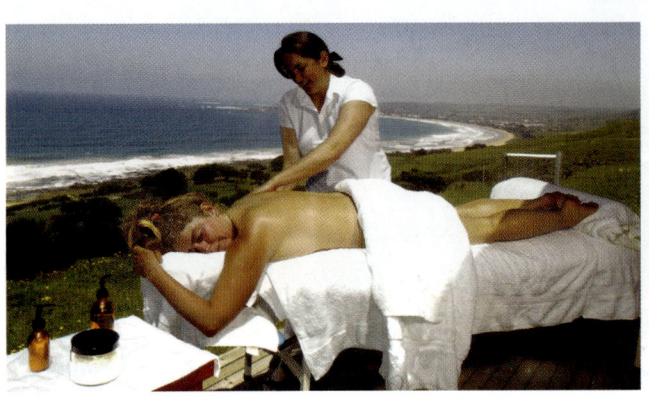

Welcome to Seafarers Getaway - Apollo Bay's sensational beach retreat where the country meets the coast. Enjoy 6 star views from our self-contained lodges and units. Visit www.seafarers.com.au for special packages.

Seafarers Getaway

6080 Great Ocean Road
Apollo Bay, Victoria 3233
Ph: (03) 5237 6507
info@seafarers.com.au
www.seafarers.com.au

- The Otway National Park has facilities including water, picnic tables, fireplaces and toilets. Camping is not permitted but accommodation is available in nearby Lavers Hill, Beech Forest and Johanna.

COMING & GOING
- Lorne to Apollo Bay: 45km, 50min
- Apollo Bay to Port Campbell: 96km, 1.20hr.

NATURAL ATTRACTIONS
- Many plants in this rainforest gully grow on trees, including kangaroo fern, weeping spleenwort and shiny shield-fern. These are epiphytes and survive on decaying leaves and bark. Another unusual local is the glossy black-shelled snail, a carnivorous species unique to the Otways. The snails can be seen along the track in wet weather.

MORE INFO
- Various professionally guided activities are offered in the Otway National Park, including bird watching, bushwalking, car and limousine tours, bus tours, 4WD tours and spotlight tours and night walks. For further details contact Parks Victoria Ph: 131 963 Web: www.parkweb.vic.gov.au The visitor information centre When: 9am–5pm daily Where: on Apollo Bay foreshore Ph: (03) 5237 6529 Web: www.visitapollobay.com

MELBA GULLY

MELBA GULLY
Melba Gully was purchased for Mrs Jessie Fry in 1921 and named by her after Australia's famous singer, Dame Nellie Melba. Through the 1930s and 1940s Melba Gully was a popular picnic and lunch stop for bus tourists, but this stopped in 1948 when a length limit was imposed on buses using Otway roads. The beauty of Melba Gully more than fits its local description as the Jewel of the Otways, made especially sparkling by its resident glow-worms. One of the wettest areas in the state, with an annual rainfall of over 2000mm, the gully is a dense rainforest of myrtle, beech, blackwood and tree ferns carpeted by low ferns and mosses — all surviving remnants of the ancient Otways rainforest. The current picnic area is on the site of what was Mrs Fry's tearooms. The large open area was established as a farm and is being gradually revegetated with indigenous species like mountain ash. In 1958 the property was sold to Mr and Mrs Axel Madsen, who donated it to the Victorian Conservation Trust in 1975. It is now managed by Parks Victoria Where: Melba Gully State Park is 1.5km off the GOR and about 3km west of Lavers Hill. The access road is narrow and steep in places but suitable for conventional vehicles.

Superb, contemporary Bed and Breakfast in the Heart of town. Relaxed and friendly style. Renowned as more than a B&B.

Captain's At The Bay

21 Pascoe St
Apollo Bay, Victoria 3233
Ph: (03) 5237 6771 Fax: (03) 5237 7337
captains@vicnet.net.au
www.captains.net.au

THE OTWAYS

More than a mountain range the Otways takes in some of Victoria's most spectacular and unspoiled landscapes. Rich in fossils, the Otway Range was formed 150 million years ago when dinosaurs roamed the earth and the great southern land known as Gondwana began to break up.

OTWAY NATIONAL PARK

Within a 60km stretch from Apollo Bay to Princetown, near the Twelve Apostles, lies some of Victoria's most rugged coastline and spectacular rainforest. Accessible from the Great Ocean Road, the Otway National Park (12 876ha) has 36 species of native mammals, including the Australian fur seal, as well as swamp wallabies, koalas and eastern grey kangaroos.

The park is ideal for a variety of outdoor activities from leisurely walks to more extensive and adventurous hiking and exploration. Along the way, observe the dense tree ferns and towering myrtle beech trees.

Further along the coast, Cape Otway contains some of the Great Ocean Road's wildest terrain. On the most southerly point of the road, a short drive from Apollo Bay stands one of Australia's oldest lighthouses built in 1848, following numerous shipwrecks along this treacherous stretch of coast. A telegraph station and keepers' cottages are within in the lightstation precinct.

The cape is a national park and the Victorian government recently added another 100 000ha, extending the park all the way to Anglesea, further protecting the largely unspoilt coastline and native animals. The Otways contains many and varied waterfalls. The most accessible include Hopetoun, Beauchamp and Stevenson waterfalls and are a must see for visitors. The Otway Range experience the highest rainfall in Victoria with an average of 2000mm annually.

MUST SEE:

- Discover the rainforest at Maits Rest. This secluded gully of cool-temperate rainforest, just a short drive from Apollo Bay, is the place to start exploring the Otways. A short boardwalk and viewing platform allows you to experience the charm of the rainforest gullies. Watch out for the 300-year-old beech tree which is on the National Trust's historic register.

WORTH VISITING

- Visit Melba Gully. A cool-temperate rainforest near Lavers Hill, Melba Gully is one of the wettest places in Victoria. Take the 1km walk along Madsen's track and observe the intricate and ancient plant life, lush ferns, mosses and fungi. Known as the 'Jewell of the Otways', Melba Gully is home to thousands of glow-worms that light up at night. Take time to linger in this enchanting area, which has picnic and barbecue facilities.

CAN DO

- Take the Otway Fly Tree Top Walk. A 600m long, 25m high walk above the forest floor and among the rainforest tree tops — it's a great way to admire the magnificence of the Otways. A 47m-high lookout tower gives a splendid view of tall eucalypts. The Otway Fly is one of only three steel canopy walks in the world; the other two are in Western Australia and Tasmania. After the walk, enjoy a meal at the visitor centre at the entrance to the Fly
When: 9am–4.30/5pm daily
Ph: (03) 5235 9200

OTWAY NATIONAL PARK

HIGHLIGHTS BETWEEN APOLLO BAY AND PORT CAMPBELL

HOPETOUN FALLS, OTWAY NATIONAL PARK

The first part of the drive between Apollo Bay and Port Campbell is fringed by towering trees and delicate ferns as the road winds inland from Apollo Bay past Marengo and into the heart of the Otway National Park.

The Otway National Park west of Apollo Bay is a riot of rainforest and unspoilt beaches augmented by beautiful rock formations in coves like Blanket Bay. The park extends inland from Blanket Bay and Shelly Beach along the coast to Princetown.

The latter section is through rich dairy country, then the more sparse scrubland that skirts the spectacular cliffs of the Twelve Apostles Marine National Park.

MUST SEE

- Visit the park's once best-kept local secret: Maits Rest. Named after former forestry patrol officer Maitland Bryant, Maits Rest is known for its natural beauty. Experience it on the short walk that meanders through a tranquil fern glade and past huge, centuries-old moss-covered trees.

- Cape Otway is the most southerly point on the GOR and one of the most southerly spots in Victoria. The cape's ruggedness is matched by the lush rainforest surrounding it. Much of the cape is national park that protects its unspoilt coastline, rainforest and a range of native animals. Right at the tip is one of Australia's oldest lighthouses.

WORTH VISITING

- Cape Otway Lighthouse. This 20m tower was built in 1848 after a series of terrible shipwrecks near the cape. It was the second lighthouse to be built on the Australian mainland. The lighthouse guides ships bound for Port Phillip through the narrow entrance to Bass Strait. For a fee you can climb to the top and experience spectacular coastal views. You can visit briefly or organise to stay in the accommodation available on site.

- Moonlight Head. Around Moonlight Head you can see some of the highest coastal cliffs in mainland Australia. Descend the 400 steps to Wreck Beach, where anchors from the *Marie Gabrielle* and the *Fiji* (each wrecked on the rocks), are embedded in the sand Where: Turn off the GOR to Moonlight Head between Lavers Hill and Princetown. The access track passes a small cemetery with decorative gates and stonework, then forks to Wreck Beach and the Gable.

- The Gable is a lookout platform overhanging the clifftop with views of Moonlight Head and the ocean below.

CAN DO

- There are superb walks throughout the Otway National Park. For example, the waterfall reserves at Beauchamp, Hopetoun and around Triplet Falls all have well-marked dry tracks that follow picturesque valleys shaded by cathedrals of giant mountain ash. Remember to wear good walking shoes and take a raincoat.

NATURAL ATTRACTIONS

- The recently opened Great Ocean Walk takes in a 33km stretch of spectacular coastal scenery from Apollo Bay to Cape Otway Lighthouse. The walk includes rocky platforms, sheltered

www.planbooktravel.com

beaches, pristine rivers, huge forests and coastal heathland.

- The moderate three-day walk begins at Apollo Bay or Marengo Caravan Park and ends at the Cape Otway Lightstation. Ultimately it will link Apollo Bay to the Glenample Homestead near Port Campbell covering more than 90km.

CATCH A WAVE

- The GOR meets the ocean again at Glenaire and nearby Johanna. Johanna Beach is a popular surfing and fishing beach and has hosted the international Bells Beach Surf Carnival several times.

STAYING

- Secluded and peaceful, Johanna offers a range of accommodation from luxury to bush camping, as well as backpacker, B&B and self-contained options.

TWELVE APOSTLES MARINE NATIONAL PARK

The Twelve Apostles, world famous icons of the GOR, are shown to advantage by extensive boardwalks and viewing platform. The visitor experience is awe inspiring every time, but the best time of day to see these giants is around sunrise and sunset when their jagged forms and rich colours are set into stark relief by the low light.

Begin your experience at the interpretative centre, a $5.5 million building that blends with the surrounding environment and caters for the site's million-plus annual visitors. A tunnel takes you under the road to the viewing platforms.

The erosive forces that created the Twelve Apostles began their work 20 million years ago by attacking the soft limestone of the Port Campbell cliffs. This limestone was created through the build-up of skeletons of marine creatures on the sea floor. As the sea retreated, the limestone was exposed, and gradually eroded by relentless ocean waves and winds. The result is what we see today: endless cliffs and countless caves. The latter eventually became arches and when they collapsed, the 45m rock islands of the Apostles were left isolated from the shore.

This process also produced the other natural phenomena in the area, including the Razorback, Thunder Cave, the Blowhole and the Grotto.

Loch Ard Gorge is located within the Twelve Apostles Marine Park, a massive eroded 'hole' to the ocean is named after the wreck of the iron clipper *Loch Ard*, and is the site of one of the most remarkable rescues in Australian maritime history.

GREAT OCEAN ROAD AND GRAMPIANS

Fishing and Adventure Tours

Fishing:

- Snapper, Flathead, Deep-sea shark
- 17m Boat — all facilities; gear supplied

Scenic Tours: Seal colony, Lighthouse

Shipwrecks, Daily Apollo Bay Tours

Ask about our great Accommodation Deals at Great Ocean Road Beach Houses

Family, Deluxe, Executive, 1,2,3 Bedroom. FSC, Spas, Woodfires, A/C, Seaviews, Private Balconies.

Otway Lodge
23 Pascoe Street, Apollo Bay
www.otwaylodge.com.au

Bayview Apartments
46 Noel Street, Apollo Bay
www.bayviewapartments.com.au

Apollo Bay Fishing & Adventure Tours
Bookings: (03) 5237 7888 Mob: 0418 121 784
www.apollobayfishing.com.au

Great Ocean Road Beach Houses
Bookings: (03) 5237 7850 Mob: 0419 526 384
www.greatoceanrdbeachhouses.com.au

PORT CAMPBELL TO WARRNAMBOOL

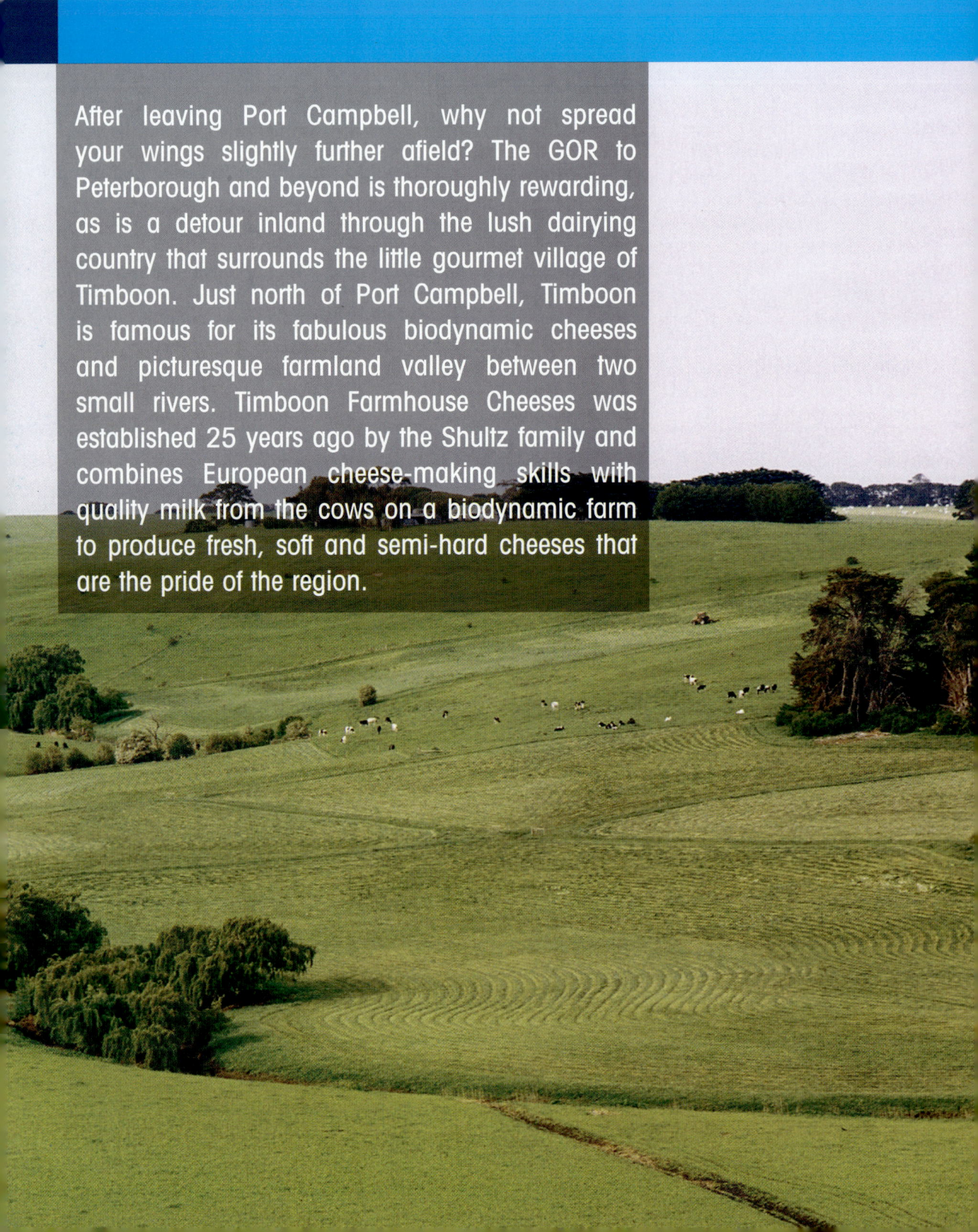

After leaving Port Campbell, why not spread your wings slightly further afield? The GOR to Peterborough and beyond is thoroughly rewarding, as is a detour inland through the lush dairying country that surrounds the little gourmet village of Timboon. Just north of Port Campbell, Timboon is famous for its fabulous biodynamic cheeses and picturesque farmland valley between two small rivers. Timboon Farmhouse Cheeses was established 25 years ago by the Shultz family and combines European cheese-making skills with quality milk from the cows on a biodynamic farm to produce fresh, soft and semi-hard cheeses that are the pride of the region.

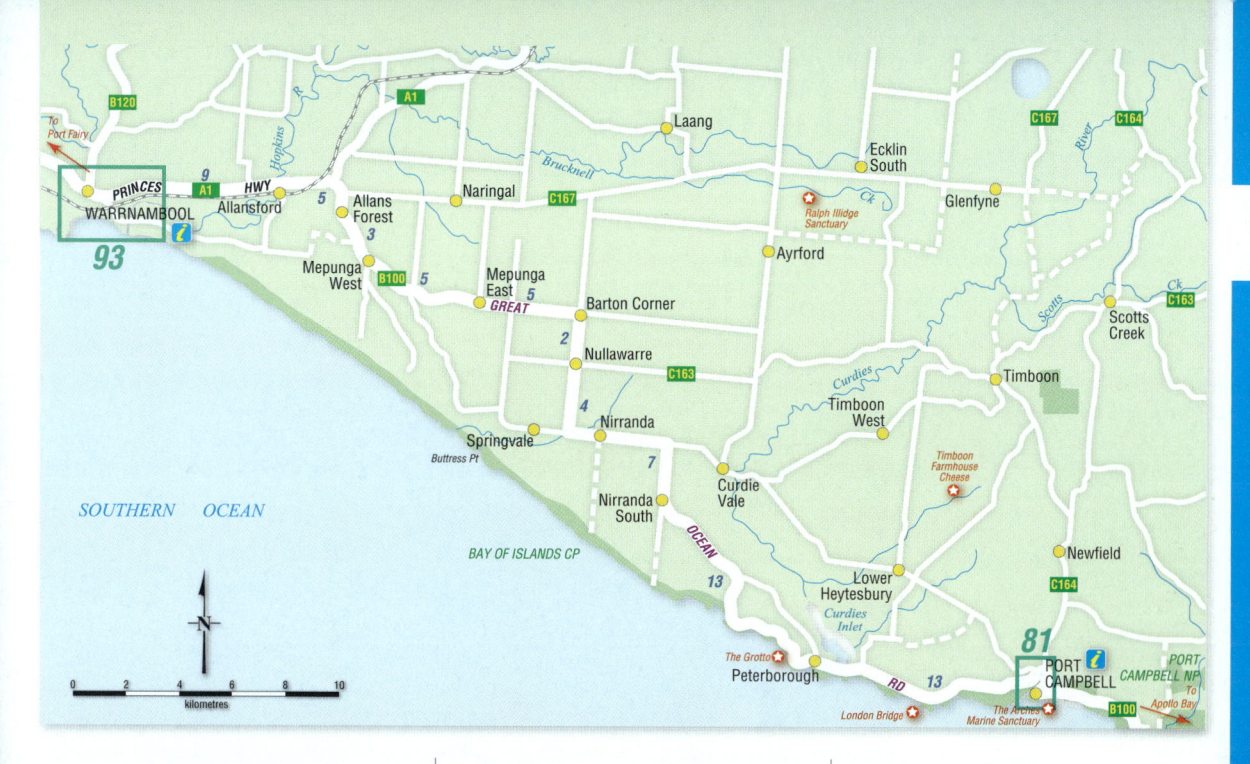

Peterborough locals are proud of their spectacular coastline, now protected within the Bay of Islands Coastal Park just outside of town. This breathtaking stretch of broad bays and coves, like the Bay of Martyrs and Massacre Bay, is every bit as breathtaking as the cliffs and crags of the Twelve Apostles. The rock stacks are smaller, but so numerous they are hard to count. In addition to the natural spectacle on display between Port Campbell and Warrnambool there are plenty of adventures for the active traveller, from leisurely pursuits like golf on the picturesque Peterborough course, to boating, fishing, surfing and bushwalking.

But remember the weather and ocean conditions are unpredictable along this coast, so exercise caution when swimming, fishing or surfing. Similarly, when sightseeing or bushwalking be aware of undermined cliff edges and keep to designated walking tracks and viewing platforms. After all, it is the treacherousness of this rugged shoreline that makes it so impressive, and accounts for so much of its remarkable and tragic history. Learn about the numerous ships that came to grief on the reefs and rocks around here and you'll understand why it was so feared by 19th century sailors. The rusting wreckage of many foundered ships still lies strewn along its length — some beaches even feature half buried anchors as sobering reminders of a dangerous time. Such visible history lends an air of mystery to an already evocative place, and when you add ample accommodation choices and great places to dine, this section of the GOR is bound to captivate.

PETERBOROUGH

PORT CAMPBELL

www.planbooktravel.com

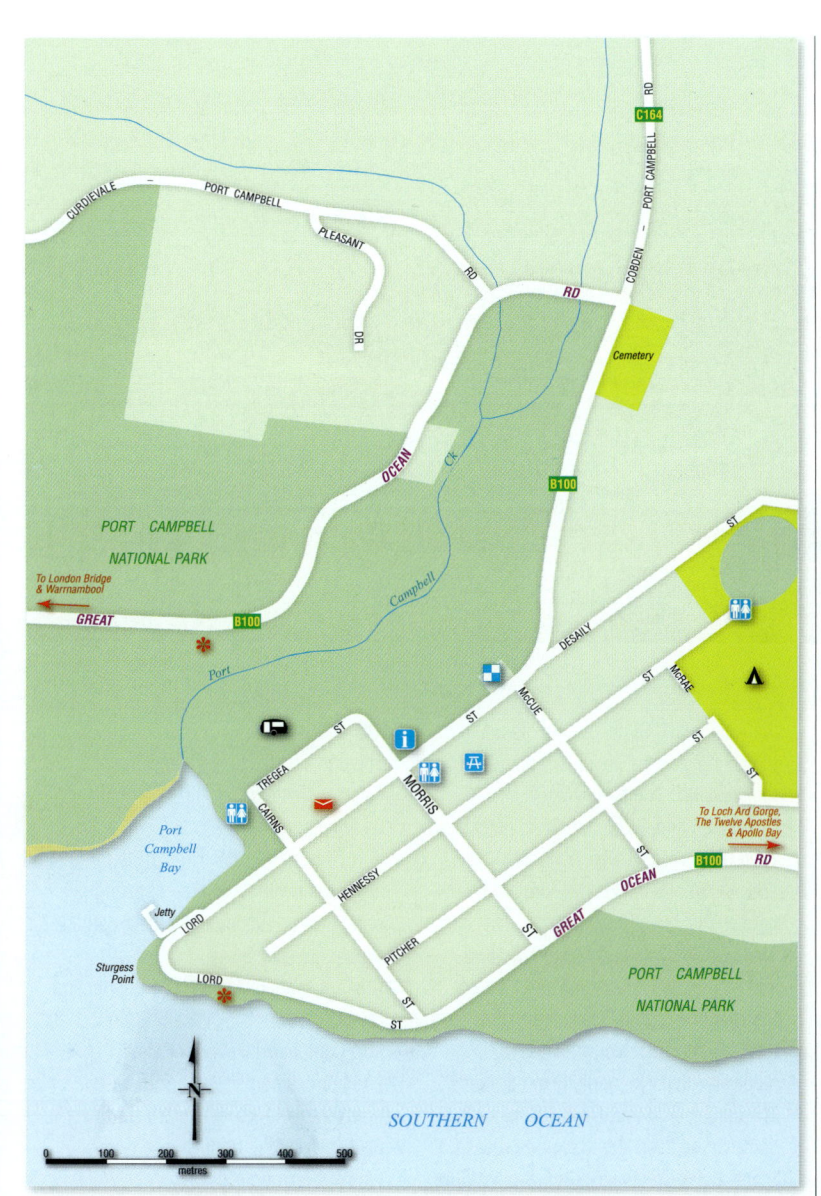

Ard Gorge, the Blowhole, The Arch and Thunder Cave. To the east of town are the sweeping beaches of Gibson Steps and beyond, just west of Peterborough, is the Bay of Islands and the Bay of Martyrs.

- Another good place to stop just before Peterborough is the Grotto, where a path leads from the clifftop to a rock pool beneath an archway. For a bird's-eye view of all the sights, take to the air with one of the scenic flight operators, like Twelve Apostles Helicopters **Where:** 9400 GOR **Ph:** (03) 5598 6161

WORTH VISITING

- The Port Campbell Trading Company is a small art gallery which shows works by local artists **Where:** 27 Lord St.
- The Loch Ard Shipwreck Museum has exhibits and videos that relay the stories of five of the shipwrecks in the region: the *Loch Ard*, *Fiji*, *Schomberg*, *Falls of Halladale* and *Newfield*. Artefacts salvaged from some of these wrecks are also on display here **When:** 9am–5pm daily **Where:** opposite the Port Campbell Trading Company on Lord St

CAN DO

- Each of these natural attractions have well marked and maintained walking tracks. The mouth of the creek and steps on each headland are also spectacular walks from Port Campbell itself. Visit the Port Campbell National Park Information Centre for details, including leaflets describing the self-guided 90min Port Campbell Discovery Walk, which traverses a clifftop to a viewpoint above Two Mile Bay **When:** 10am–5pm daily **Where:** Port Campbell National Park Information Centre, Morris St **Ph:** (03) 5598 6382

GREAT OCEAN ROAD AND GRAMPIANS

81

An ideal base from which to explore the myriad attractions of its spectacular namesake, the Port Campbell National Park, Port Campbell is a quiet coastal town perched on the rim of enormous cliffs. It has a concentration of accommodation, eateries and interesting activities which range from an informative museum to rewarding coastal walks, fishing and scuba diving.

POPULATION
460

MUST SEE

- Right on the doorstep of Port Campbell are sights including the Twelve Apostles, Loch

PORT CAMPBELL

PORT CAMPBELL

NATURAL ATTRACTIONS
- Small coastal heath flowers bloom in the bushland around Port Campbell during spring, including more than 20 varieties of native orchid, 14 lilies and 15 pea family species in the national park. For further details on the natural wonders of this area see the section on Port Campbell National Park p.86.

HISTORICAL INTERESTS
- Sealers and whalers visited this spot regularly and used the small gorge inlet at Port Campbell for shelter during voyages between Tasmania (then Van Diemens Land), King Island and Port Jackson. Captain Alexander Campbell, a Scot in charge of the Port Fairy Whaling Station, is credited with naming the small town. The town developed primarily as a small fishing port before 1900.
- A small coastal trader, *Asia*, linked the early settlement with Warrnambool before being replaced by the *Hannah Thompson* which serviced most of the ports on the west coast. Such vessels often had to wait outside the small harbour until the prevailing south-westerly winds moderated and allowed them to enter. Even then, vessels were secured with special springs to ride the surge in the narrow inlet.
- The first jetty was constructed in 1880 and around this time shipwrecks caught the attention of both scavengers and tourists. The *Loch Ard* wreck in 1878 received extensive publicity in particular. The cemetery in Port Campbell records some of the lives lost in various wrecks.
- Steps and lookouts were constructed from this time on and tourists began visiting for the coast's spectacular scenery.
- A particularly dramatic incident took place in 1990 when London Bridge collapsed. Tourists could walk across this double-arched rock formation located just west of Port Campbell. But in January 1990 the outer span collapsed and fell into the sea minutes after two people had crossed it. The pair were rescued by helicopter.

FOOD & WINE
- There is a wide choice of restaurants, cafes and eateries in Port Campbell, including:
- Port Campbell Hotel When: daily for lunch and dinner with the option of eating by open fires or outside in the beer garden Where: 40 Lord St.
- Great Australian Bite on Lord St opposite the beach.
- Port Campbell Take Away Cafe.
- Emma's Tearooms When: Thurs–Sun, from 11am–11pm Where: 25 Lord St .
- Bakers Oven and Coffeehouse opposite Emma's Tearooms.
- Visit Port Campbell General Store if you're stocking up to eat in When: open daily in winter 8am–6pm, and in summer 7am–7pm. The store also doubles as the post office and newsagent, and has EFTPOS facilities.

GO DIVE
- Diving tours from Port Campbell visit large undersea canyons and gorges just off

the coast. These are covered by colourful invertebrates which, when set waving by the current, are like watching a marine ballet. Port Campbell Marine Services leads dives to key spots and has diving and snorkelling gear for hire
When: 9am–6pm daily
Where: 32 Lord St
Ph: (03) 5598 6411

CATCH A WAVE
- Surfing is epic in this area so it is sensible to go out with someone who knows the place, unless you are highly experienced and adventurous. Two Mile Bay is considered one of the best big wave breaks in Australia. By contrast, the small sandy curve of Port Campbell beach is safe for swimming and patrolled in summer.

GO FISH
- Boat tours take anglers and passengers near the stacks, caves and arches, and they are a good way to get close to some of the coastline's impressive features. But remember, boating is limited by unpredictable seas and weather. Even the professional fishermen sometimes have to wait days before leaving the harbour.
- For details on fishing charters visit the small jetty about halfway along the inlet or contact Port Campbell Marine Services Where: 32 Lord St
Ph: (03) 5598 6411
- If you don't feel like going to sea, there is excellent fishing in Campbells Creek and other creeks, plus the harbour itself. When the swell is smaller the beaches are also great places to cast a line.

STAYING
- Take your pick of the comprehensive range of accommodation here. It ranges from affordable quality motels like the Port O'Call (37 Lord St) and the more expensive Southern Ocean Motor Inn (also on Lord St, and featuring a licensed restaurant) to B&B options, farmstays and the Port Campbell National Park Cabin and Caravan Park (on Tregea St), which offers on-site vans and beachside cabins.

WHAT'S ON
Jan: Swim Series, open ocean race in sheltered Port Campbell Bay; Timboon Railway Music Festival
Mar: Breakfast with the Twelve Apostles, cooked breakfast sampling the good local produce.

MORE INFO
- Visitor information centre
When: 9am–5pm daily
Where: 26 Morris St
Ph: (03) 55986053
Web: www.visit12apostles.com

COMING & GOING
- Port Campbell to Warrnambool 66km

CAFE OVERLOOKING BAY, PORT CAMPBELL

PORT CAMPBELL SHOPS

SHIPWRECKS

Few coastlines have proved as disastrous for shipping. Not just the aptly-named shipwreck coast between Peterborough and Apollo Bay either, there were almost as many wrecks and loss of life east of Cape Otway. Over a period of 200 years more than 600 ships went to the bottom, and hundreds of lives went with them. But it was never worse than in the 1850s goldrushes. A rapid rise in ship numbers resulted in an equivalent spate of disasters. The following is an outline of some of the tragic tales that have unfolded along this treacherous coast.

CASINO

A terrible tale in a stormy Apollo Bay harbour took place on the morning of 10 July, 1932. In only three hours the sea had claimed 10 lives; one women, a child and eight crew (including the captain) from the steamship *Casino*. A veteran of the coastal trade with more than 50 years service, the ship was carrying two passengers, 17 crew and 240 tons of cargo. Berthing was impossible so the captain headed for deeper water to wait out the storm. But the anchor punched a large hole in the vessel's keel plate, causing the ship to roll on its side and sink broadside to the waves near shore.

CITY OF RAYVILLE

The first American vessel sunk in WWII went down in the icy waters off Cape Otway in November 1940. The lighthouse keeper raised the alarm when he saw an orange flash and heard an explosion. *The City of Rayville* was almost certainly struck by a German mine (with the loss of one life) as no Australian or British mines had been laid. A secret Australian naval report at the time mentions a British ship sunk the previous day in a similar manner.

FIJI

One of the most sensational and spectacular wrecks along the Victorian coast. The *Fiji* was a 230ft barque that foundered in bad weather during September 1891, claiming 12 lives. Carrying cargo that included 200 tons of dynamite, the ship hit rocks less than 300m from shore near Wreck Beach and the cliffs of Moonlight Head. But the ship didn't sink, and rescuers from Warrnambool and Port Campbell managed to save most on board. Scavengers took a lot of cargo that washed up on the beach, including cases of gin and brandy, toys and cakes of dynamite. Today you can still see the *Fiji's* anchor embedded in the sands of Wreck Beach. The wreck itself is dangerous and divers should be extremely cautious.

CAPE OTWAY LIGHTHOUSE

SHIPPING RELIC IN WARRNAMBOOL

LOCH ARD

The dramatic loss of the *Loch Ard* in June 1878 is a story of tragedy, luck and considerable heroism. This three-masted iron clipper left England in March that year with 51 passengers and crew, and a fortune in cargo. Three months later fog and haze prevented the captain correctly calculating the pass into Bass Strait — a task so critical and difficult it was called 'threading the eye of the needle'.

When the fog lifted on the morning of 1 June, the towering cliffs appeared only a short distance away. Despite evasive action by dropping anchors the ship hit the reef and sank 15min later.

Only two people survived: 18 year-old crewman, Tom Pierce, and passenger Eva Carmichael, also 18, who was travelling to Australia with her family. Both were washed into a deep gorge now named after the *Loch Ard*. Eva couldn't swim but used a chicken coop and a spar to stay afloat. Tom swam to her in the waves and after a struggle, got her safely into a cave at the end of the gorge. He then went for help, running into a party from nearby Glenample station, which returned to the gorge to rescue Eva.

Today you can see where this disaster took place, walk on the beach, and see the monument to the Carmichael family in the clifftop cemetery. Glenample Homestead has extensive displays that tell the *Loch Ard* story. It is closed Tues and Fri.

MARIE

Not much is known about the last hours of the *Marie*, lost in violent seas off rugged Cape Bridgewater in September 1851. Nearly a month passed before reports of the disaster circulated in the district. The barque was on a voyage from Antwerp to Sydney via Adelaide with 25 passengers and crew, including the Belgian consul and his staff. All on board were lost, but the circumstances of the wreck remain a mystery.

SACRAMENTO

This three-masted sailing ship was only three years old when it struck the Point Lonsdale reef at the notoriously dangerous entrance into Port Phillip in April 1853. En route to Melbourne from London and carrying more than 300 passengers and crew, the *Sacramento* came to grief when it drifted towards shore in the middle of the night. Everyone was rescued but the ship quickly broke up. Within a week the hull had snapped in two, littering nearby beaches with wreckage.

JOSEPH H. SCAMMELL

The wrecking of this American ship on a reef near Point Danger at Torquay in May 1891 resulted in some of the most extensive looting and smuggling on the Victorian coast. After rounding Cape Otway on a voyage from New York to Melbourne, the *Scammell* was caught in strong currents and dragged onto the reef. Word spread about the wreck and despite the best attempts of customs and police officers to stop them, thousands of scavengers began stealing the spoils that littered the beaches for kilometres. Some even buried goods in nearby paddocks. A Geelong local bought the wreck and auctioned it on the beach only a week after the ship foundered. What was left of the valuable cargo was sold for a fraction of its original price. One participant even bought the wheelhouse and incorporated it into a Torquay house.

SCHOMBERG

One of the most magnificent sailing vessels ever built, the *Schomberg*'s maiden voyage in 1885 was also its last. The expensive ship was expected to break all speed records on the England to Australia run, especially under the command of James 'Bully' Forbes, a captain known for putting ship speed before the comfort of passengers. But 81 days into the voyage *Schomberg* was near shore at Peterborough (with Forbes playing cards below deck) when it struck a reef. All were evacuated and the ship finally broke up in January the following year. A decade later, attempts to recover the cargo resulted in two drownings.

PORT CAMPBELL NATIONAL PARK

Famous for the Twelve Apostles and a remarkable number of historic shipwrecks, Port Campbell National Park contains the most significant areas of flora and fauna native to south-western Victoria. Its diverse range of coastal environments include woodlands, dunes, wetlands, coastal cliffs, limestone stacks and arches.

MUST SEE
- Various scenic drives along the GOR with numerous stops at points of interest. Three self-guided walks at Loch Ard Gorge that introduce shipwreck history, geology and coastal ecology.
- Visit historic Glenample Homestead where the two survivors of the Loch Ard shipwreck were taken after their rescue.
- During summer, watch the thousands of short-tailed shearwaters (mutton birds) that return to their nest burrows from the sea each evening.
- Tackle the Port Campbell Discovery Walk that heads west from the township of Port Campbell.
- Swim, surf, fish, snorkel and scuba dive at Port Campbell. Take advantage of the numerous tours.

WORTH VISITING
- Built from local sandstone in 1869 by pioneer pastoralist Hugh Gibson, Glenample Homestead now houses rewarding displays on the *Loch Ard* tragedy and early station life. Picnic facilities are provided in the garden
When: 11am–4pm every day Dec–Mar and throughout Easter.
Ph: (03) 5598 8209
- Visit Loch Ard Cemetery on the clifftop above Loch Ard Gorge. Four victims of the wreck of the Loch Ard are buried here.

CAN DO
- Various guided activities are available within the park, these include coastal and bushwalking, spotlight tours, night walks, bird watching, bicycle touring, boat and fishing tours, sea kayaking and 4WD tours.

NATURAL ATTRACTIONS
- Despite being relatively small and narrow, the park plays an all-important role in the conservation of the region's fauna. It supports populations of the hooded plover (a nationally-significant species), rufous bristlebird, swamp antechinus and glossy grass skink. Established tea-tree heathlands are vital to the rufous bristlebird, while wetland areas provide food and nesting sites for the Australasian bittern, Lewin's rail and swamp skink. Eastern grey kangaroos shelter in the park's denser vegetation but often feed in nearby farmland.
- The park features remnant coastal vegetation types, including important coastal heathlands, shrubby sand dunes, clifftop grasslands and shrublands, open forests, woodlands and swamps.
- Each supports a remarkable range of important plants, including the swamp greenhood, clover glycine, square raspwort, lime fern and metallic sun-orchid. Because much of the native vegetation no longer exists outside the park, these plants are of real significance in the region.

HISTORICAL INTERESTS
- Aboriginal people spent considerable time along this shore cutting steps down the sheer cliffs to access the ocean's abundance of seafood. European explorers quickly realised the coastline's dangers and kept well clear. Even so, shipwreck numbers kept increasing and the treacherous stretch soon earned the title of The Shipwreck Coast. Early settlement in the region was predominantly pastoral, with runs like Glenample established along the coast, and a small fishing port at Port Campbell.

STAYING
- There is no camping in the park but you can stay at the Port Campbell Camping and Caravan Park, or at any of the other diverse accommodation options in town.

PROTECTING THE PARK
- Stay on tracks and boardwalks at all times. Please take rubbish away with you. Fires are not permitted. Dogs and other pets aren't permitted, except for dogs in cars on the main tourist roads. Camping and sleeping overnight in vehicles in the park are not permitted. Please do not disturb or remove any plants or animals. Visit the Port Campbell National Park Information Centre in Port Campbell for more detailed information on the park, or contact Parks Victoria.
Web: www.parkweb.vic.gov.au
Ph: 131 963

THE PARKS INFORMATION CENTRE

HIGHLIGHTS BETWEEN PORT CAMPBELL AND WARRNAMBOOL

THE BRIDGE TO PETERBOROUGH

The drive between Port Campbell and Warrnambool offers plenty of options, although not all in the same direction. Follow the GOR along the cliff-lined coast to Peterborough or head inland to tantalise your taste buds in nearby Timboon, the small town famous for its fabulous cheeses.

WORTH VISITING
- Peterborough is 13km west of Port Campbell on the GOR. While the road skirts the town centre and the river mouth here, both deserve to be explored. Here Curdies River widens into a broad estuary perfect for fishing, bird watching or simply taking the air. The spectacular shoreline is augmented by views of tiny islands and rocky outcrops along the beach. Out to sea to the east is Schomberg Rock which marks the wreck of the *Schomberg*. Take a stroll to the lookout by the river mouth for great views across Newfield Bay and the fantastically shaped cliffs.

NATURAL ATTRACTIONS
- The Port Campbell National Park is easy to access from Peterborough. Well maintained tracks wind through this flat coastal heathland along the clifftops. Beyond Peterborough the road heads inland, but take your time because you're passing the Bay of Islands Coastal Park, a 32km stretch of protected heathland habitat for rare and threatened flora and fauna, against a spectacular ocean backdrop. Access to the Bay of Islands Coastal Park is at the eastern (Peterborough) end, beginning at Wild Dog Cove.
- The Bay of Islands and the Bay of Martyrs nearby both feature rock stacks in the sea like the Twelve Apostles, but they are shorter and there are more of them. This coastline has a character all its own. It seems to close in around you, with many curved cliffs and bays filled with rock towers. Several accessible smaller bays like Worm Bay, Crofts Bay, Boat Bay, and in the western section of the park, Childers Cove, also offer magnificent views and secluded beaches.
- Don't miss the sunset over the Bay of Islands — every bit as beautiful and romantic as it sounds.

HISTORICAL INTERESTS
- Timboon — the town's name apparently comes from the local Aboriginal word, 'timboun', which described the pieces of rock used to open mussels. Timboon was first settled in the late 1870s but didn't prosper until the railway arrived from Camperdown in 1892. The timber industry thrived here, with as many as 18 mills processing 132 000 tons of wood in a year. Lime kilns by the old railway in Timboon produced lime for

cement throughout the district. All this early industry led to the building of Victoria's first consolidated school. But sheep and dairy farming were the principal pursuits of the region and, in 1955, the Heytesbury Settlement Scheme resulted in more than 160 000ha of forest being cleared for dairy farms. The village of Simpson just to the east displays equipment used for this vast undertaking.

- Sealers and whalers regularly visited the coast around Peterborough from 1800 onward, but they didn't stay, preferring the shelter of the inlet at nearby Port Campbell. In 1840, Dr D. Curdie took up property at Tandarook, a few kilometres upstream from the mouth of the small stream, later named after him. The area of present day Peterborough was occupied in 1846 by Duncan Hoyle with other settlers following. A township was proclaimed in 1886. In 1855 a larger clipper, *Schomberg*, was caught on a reef near the inlet on her maiden voyage from England (due to navigational error). The passengers were rescued but the ship broke up. The three-masted schooner, *Young Australia*, was also wrecked near the inlet about 20 years later, followed by the *Newfield* in 1892 and the *Falls of Halladale* in 1908.

CAN DO

- Much of the coastline between Peterborough and Warrnambool is connected by good walking tracks and is ideal for exploring. Other rugged beaches include Massacre Bay and the more isolated Childers Cove. Massacre Bay is a popular surfing and fishing beach, but take care in the often treacherous waters Explore the Ralph Illidge Sanctuary 25km north of Peterborough. Visit Warrnambool Visitor Information Centre for details.

FOOD & WINE

- Timboon is known for a range of biodynamic cheeses, including Camembert and Brie, made just south of town by Timboon Farmhouse Cheeses. These cheeses continue to receive awards in Australia and internationally. Farmhouse Cheeses were among the first to be made without the aid of chemicals. The Camembert, Brie, triple cream and Buetten are absolute 'must tries', preferably with a drop of good Victorian wine **When:** Cheese shop open 10am–4pm daily **Where:** cnr of Ford and Fells Rds, Timboon. **Ph:** (03) 5598 3387

GO BOATING

- There is an ocean boat ramp at the carpark by the river mouth, and a boat ramp north of the bridge (just past the caravan park). The river and inlet are shallow with a single deep channel. The coves around Peterborough are protected from most winds.

TEE OFF

- Peterborough has a challenging nine-hole golf course with stunning ocean views. For more information contact Peterborough Golf Club
Ph: (03) 5598 5245

BREAKS & DETOURS

- Located less than 20km to the north of Port Campbell, Timboon is set in a picturesque valley of bushland and dairy farms threaded by two small watercourses, Curdies River and Scotts Creek. There are limestone caves in the region; for details ask at Port Campbell Visitor Information Centre before setting off. Cross into town over the Curdies River via a beautiful old trestle railway bridge. Built in 1892, the bridge is made of bush timber poles and is a rarity these days, with few examples still existing in Victoria. The old Timboon Post Office site is another reminder of a bygone age. Enjoy a picnic at the Flora and Fauna Reserve or the picnic ground near the Curdies River bridge.

BAY OF ISLANDS, PORT CAMPBELL

WARRNAMBOOL TO PORTLAND

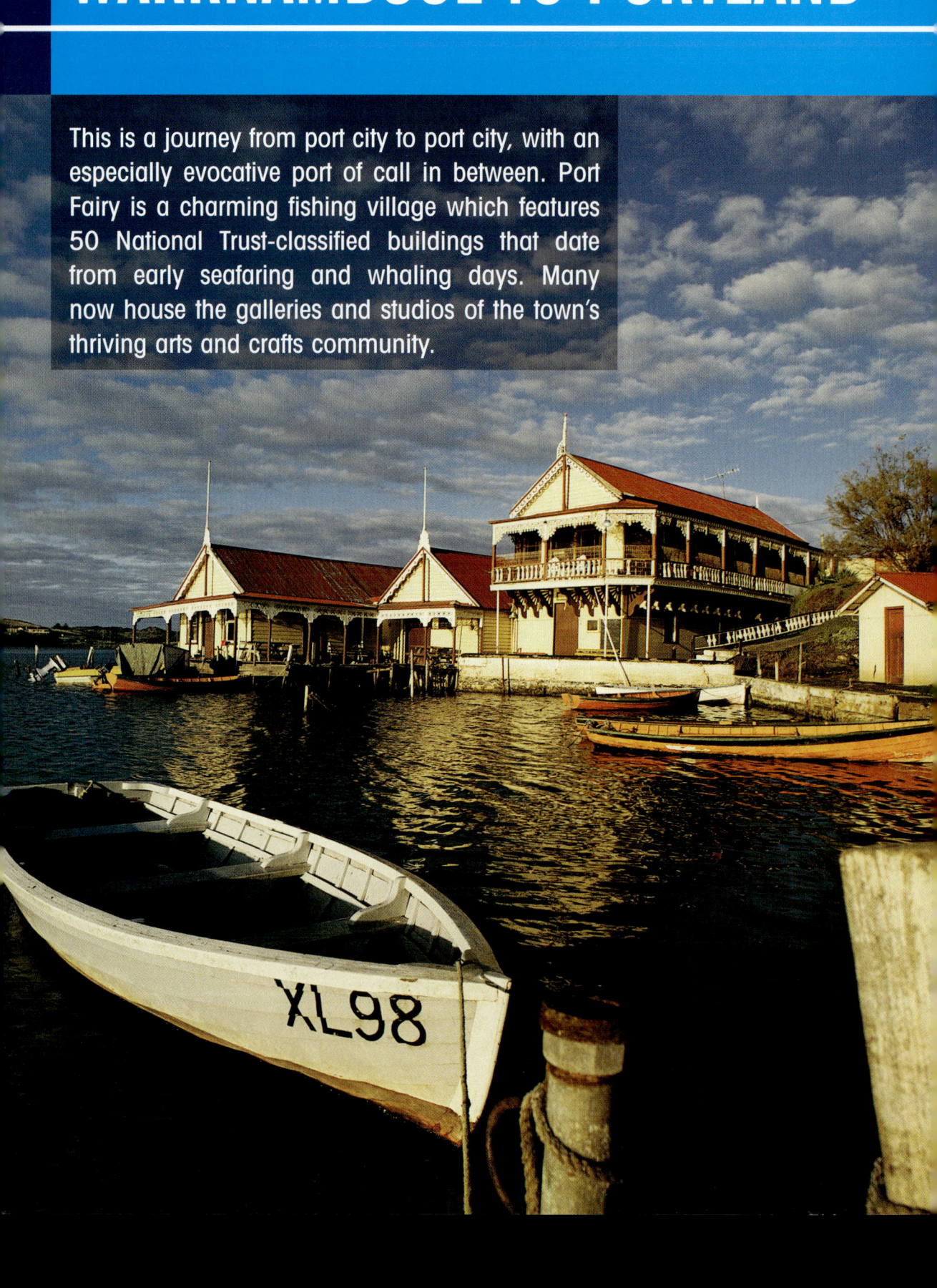

This is a journey from port city to port city, with an especially evocative port of call in between. Port Fairy is a charming fishing village which features 50 National Trust-classified buildings that date from early seafaring and whaling days. Many now house the galleries and studios of the town's thriving arts and crafts community.

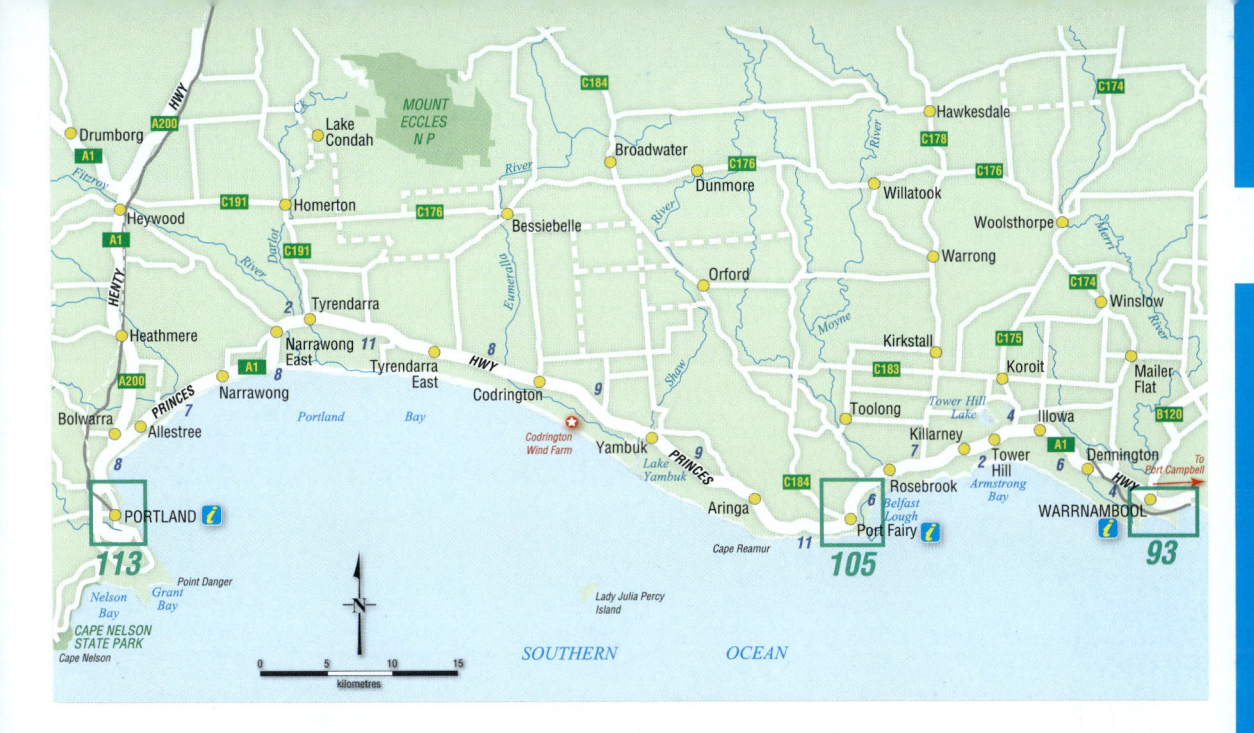

Replete with rugged coastlines and secluded swimming beaches, the step-back-in-time appeal of Port Fairy is enhanced by its place as one of Victoria's oldest operational fishing ports. Take a wander around the postcard-perfect harbour where the local fishing fleet shelters, often moored alongside visiting shark, squid and scallop boats, depending on the season. It is difficult to resist snapping endless photos here, especially when the Moyne River's calm waters reflect a kaleidoscope of colourful boat hulls, stone buildings and striking Norfolk pines. But this isn't necessarily what makes Port Fairy famous. Music lovers descend in droves for the international Port Fairy Folk Festival held annually in March, plus various other national music festivals throughout the year. On the way to Port Fairy, take a slight detour north to the tiny hinterland town of Koroit.

Here rich black volcanic soils support potato growing, first started by Irish settlers who arrived during Ireland's potato famine in the 1840s. Today Koroit has a National Trust classification for its authentic streetscapes, especially the Mickey Bourke's Hotel, which is known for its lively St Patrick's Day celebrations. If you're in town at the time, stop and sip green ale with the friendly locals.

Get the lie of the land by ascending Tower Hill, an extinct volcano crater just outside Port Fairy. The Tower Hill State Game Reserve was Victoria's First National Park and has many lovely walking tracks and idyllic spots for barbecues, picnics or just relaxing. It's such a relaxing spot and the plethora of native wildlife is an additional bonus.

For sightseeing of a different sort beyond Port Fairy, take a tour of fascinating Codrington Wind Farm. At the time of its construction, Codrington's battery of enormous wind turbines made up Australia's largest wind power station. You'll be entranced by the professional commentary on the development of the wind farm and the technical details of those enormous turbines.

Southern right whales are seasonally on show along the coastline between Warrnambool and Portland. They are often seen cavorting just off-shore in the expanse of Portland Bay. Keep your eye out for these impressive giants as you drive around the bay into Portland.

THE VIEW FROM TOWER HILL

WARRNAMBOOL

Famous for its whale-watching opportunities, Warrnambool is a rural centre with a thriving artist community, rich history, and a growing number of attractions for tourists.

POPULATION
30 000

MUST SEE
- Visit Flagstaff Hill. Part maritime museum, and part theme park, it charts the often frightening experiences of the earlier generations of settlers who came to Australia on ships. Also at Flagstaff Hill is the sound and laser show 'Shipwrecked' (*see* Flagstaff Hill/Shipwrecked feature p.99).
- Watch whales, including southern right whales, which arrive in Warrnambool's Logans Beach to calve from May/Jun to Sept (*see* Whales feature p.98).

WORTH VISITING
- Take the youngsters to the Lake Pertobe Park and Adventure Playground adjacent to the waterfront of Warrnambool's Lady Bay. Have fun on the huge slides, flying foxes and mazes (free), or just stroll around the lake. Bring supplies and make the most of the large sheltered picnic areas and barbecues.
- The beach awaits: Lady Bay is more secluded than Logans Beach, and perfect for families. Surf patrols operate at Lady Bay during summer.
- Stroll along the Foreshore Promenade, a 5.7km track stretching from Warrnambool's famous Breakwater to Logans Beach Whale Platform.
- Visit Fletcher Jones Garden. Named after the manufacturer of quality, conservative clothing that began its operations in Warrnambool, the park contains colourful flowerbeds, a waterfall and wishing well, as well as the original hawker's wagon that Mr Fletcher Jones used when he began his enterprise. Accessed from the Princes Hwy.
- Have a cultural experience at Warrnambool Art Gallery. The collection features European Salon paintings, Melbourne Modernism (1930–50),

CYCLING ALONG THE FORESHORE PROMENADE

WARRNAMBOOL

SHOPPING ON LIEBIG STREET

NATURAL ATTRACTIONS

- Check out the rugged beauty of the coastline from Thunder Point, off MacDonald St.
- Head to Stingray Bay at the mouth of the Merri River. The bay, accessed from the end of Pertobe Rd, features rocky cliffs, rock pools, rock formations and a series of small islands. At low tide you can cross over to the Middle Island where there is a small colony of penguins.
- Head to Hopkins Falls — the Western District's 'mini-Niagara' — just 13km north-east of the city.
- The Hopkins River mouth known as 'blue mouth' offers clifftop views, rock pools and fishing opportunities.
- Find out what an extinct volcano looks like. Walk, picnic, and spot wildlife at Tower Hill State Game Reserve.
- Stroll through the Botanic Gardens. Designed in 1879 by William Guilfoyle, who also designed the Melbourne Botanic Gardens. Huge old trees, wide pathways, a fernery, band rotunda and lily pond with ducks are some of the features of the gardens When: 7am–sunset Where: Cockman St.

HISTORICAL INTERESTS

- Discover colonial-era military concerns at Cannon Hill, on Liebig St. As the name would suggest, this is a hill on which cannons had been placed. This measure was taken in 1850s to repel invading forces, which have yet to materialise. There is also a memorial to early (1500s) Portuguese exploration.
- See a monument to the first white women buried in the area. You will find 'Granny's Grave' off Hickford Pde.
- Check out the National Trust-Classified Wollaston Bridge. Built by a pastoralist in 1890, it is part of Wollaston Rd, and crosses the Merri River.
- Look at exhibits of photographs and

and contemporary–Australian paintings When: 10am-5pm Mon–Fri, noon-5pm weekends, closed Christmas Day and Good Friday Ph: (03) 5564 7832
- See more art at the Customs House Gallery, which displays contemporary art in a historic building When: 11am–5pm Thurs–Sun Where: Giles St Ph: (03) 5564 8963
- View paintings, prints, cards, and if you are lucky, whales at the Robert Ulmann Studio overlooking the ocean When: 9am–5pm most days or by appointment Where: 440 Hopkins Point Rd Ph: (03) 5565 1444

CAN DO

- Enjoy a horse trail ride along the beach Ph: (03) 5529 23(03) Web: www.rundellshr.com.au.

www.planbooktravel.com

FUN 4 KIDS FESTIVAL

documents from the past at History House **When:** 1.30pm–3:30pm Mon–Tues, 2pm–4pm first Sun of the month and every Sun in Jan **Where:** Giles St.

INDIGENOUS CULTURE

- Worn Gundidj Aboriginal Co-operative is a non-profit organisation operating at the Natural History Centre at the Tower Hill State Game Park. There you will find screen prints and other indigenous crafts on sale **Ph:** (03) 5561 5315 @: worngundidj@datafast.net.au

WHAT'S ON

Jan: Antiques and Collectables Fair, Warrnambool Showgrounds; Surf to Surf Fun Run/ Walk; Grand Annual Sprintcar Classic, Premier Speedway
Feb: Portuguese Festival (biennial 2007)
Feb/Mar: Wunta Fiesta (wine, food, music)
Apr: Easter Sprintcar Trail, Premier Speedway
May: Racing Carnival and Grand Annual Steeplechase
May: Koroit Irish Festival, Koroit
Jun: Fun 4 Kids International Festival, (award winning)
Jun/Jul: Warrnambool Artists' Society Art Show, Merri View Gallery
Oct: Agricultural Show
Nov: City of Warrnambool Art Show
Dec: Carols by Candlelight.

MOVIES

- Capitol Cinema Centre shows popular films currently in release **Where:** Kepler St **Ph:** (03) 5562 2709

RETAIL THERAPY

- Relieve your shopping mall withdrawal symptoms at the Gateway Plaza, and adjacent Harvey Norman Centre. You will see these as you head into Warrnambool (from Port Campbell) on the Princes Hwy.

MARKET TO MARKET

- An undercover market has 60–100 stalls **When:** 8.30am–1pm Sun **Where:** The showground on Koroit St.
- Spend part of your Sunday at the Hillside Market **When:** 9am–1pm weekly from 2nd Sun in Oct–Dec **Where:** Wannon Rooms at the showground in Koroit St.
- Visit the Summer Night Market at the Breakwater **When:** Fri evenings in Jan **Ph:** (03) 5562 7030.
- For fresh produce shop at the Grower's Market **When:** 8am–noon on the first Sat of the month Jan–May **Where:** Civic Green **Ph:** (03) 5562 7030

GREAT OCEAN ROAD AND GRAMPIANS

WARRNAMBOOL

FOOD & WINE
- While exploring the Flagstaff Hill complex, satisfy your hunger at the stylish Pippies by the Bay cafe and restaurant
  When: 12pm–2:30pm daily, from 6pm, breakfast available on weekends and Public Holidays
  Ph: (03) 5561 2188
  @: pippiesbythebay@bigpond.com
- Lunch at the restored Proudfoots on the Hopkins River Where: Simpson St
  Ph: (03) 5561 5055
- Enjoy the cafe culture on Liebig St.

TEE OFF
- Take the clubs to Warrnambool Golf Club's 18-hole course. Green fee is reduced after 5pm daylight saving and after 3pm eastern standard time or on Sun after 2pm. There is a pro-shop at the club and a licensed clubroom
  Where: Younger St Ph: (03) 5562 2108
  @: wbgolf@datafast.net.au
  Web: www.wgcinc.com.au

GO FISH
- The Hopkins River, above and below the falls, is a popular fishing spot. You can catch mulloway, bream, mullet and estuary perch; the upper Hopkins yields brown trout. You can try surf fishing at the mouth of the river.
- The Merri River yields bream and is renowned as a brown trout stream.
- Charter a fishing boat from 3 to 8 hours. Hiring fee includes rods, reels, tackle and bait Ph: (03) 5562 5044 or 0419 349 058 @: charters@southernrightcharters.com.au
  Web: www.southernrightcharters.com.au
- Fishing licences are available from Cycles and Fishing Plus in Liebig St; Henna St Milk Bar; Nicholson St Milk Bar; and Southern Right Fishing & Charters.
- Make life easier: head to the trout farm on Wollaston Rd, where you are guaranteed a catch. All equipment is supplied, and staff will even clean the fish for you When: 10.30am–5pm, check for winter and off-peak times
  Ph: (03) 5562 7772 or 0409 943 396

There are many more events in and around Warrnambool every year. Pick up a copy of *What's on in Warrnambool* from the visitor information centre.

BIRDING
- The Tower Hill Game Park contains many bird species, including chestnut teal, spoonbills, musk ducks, geese and other waterbirds. There is a bird hide near the Natural History Centre.

CATCH A WAVE
- Although it is much too rough for swimmers, Levy's Point is a great spot for experienced surfers (as well as anglers). Beware of dangerous rips. Access off Swinton St. Sheltered Lady Bay and Stingray Bay are safe swimming areas.
- Logans Beach is famous for whale watching, and it's also a worthy destination for surfers.

STAYING
- For cottages (ensuites), cabins or grassed campsites, check in at Surfside Holiday Park. Next to Lake Pertobe Adventure Park, the location provides perfect beach access
  Where: 1/2 Pertobe Rd
  Ph: (03) 5559 4700
  @: alewis@warrnambool.vic.gov.au
- Try Manor Gums in Mailors Flat
  Where: 170 Shady Lane, Mailors Flat
  Ph: (03) 5565 4410
  @: manorgum@hotkey.net.au
  Web: www.standard.net.au/~manorgum/main

MORE INFO
- Warrnambool Visitor Information Centre
  When: 9am-5pm daily
  Where: Flagstaff Hill, Merri St

CATCHING WAVES IN WARRNAMBOOL

www.planbooktravel.com

GREAT OCEAN ROAD AND GRAMPIANS

ALAN MARSHALL DISCOVERY TRAIL

Indulge your literary spirit: take a 45min drive to Noorat, for the Alan Marshall Discovery Trail. Marshall is the celebrated author of many works, including his most famous, *I Can Jump Puddles*, the story of his determination to beat polio. Marshall resided in Noorat in the early decades of the twentieth century.

Gain insight into Marshall's writings by touring the places that helped inspire them. The trail, designed by the Corangamite Arts Council @: mountnoorat@gatewaybbs.com.au, takes you to Marshall's former home, school, church, and other important locations. Leaflets with maps are available from the visitor information centre in Warrnambool. Head along the Princes Hwy to Terang, and then turn left at Terang–Mortlake Rd. Along the way, stop off at Terang and wander down its leafy streets and browse through its shops.

DINING ON FLAGSTAFF HILL

Ph: (03) 5564 7837 or 1800 637 725
Web: www.visitwarrnambool.com
- The City Council has a tourism section
Web: www.warrnambool.vic.gov.au

BREAKS & DETOURS

- Interact with the animals at the Cudgee Creek Wildlife Park. This 3ha property has deer, wallabies, kangaroos, emus and monkeys Where: Trotters Lane, Cudgee about 17km from Warrnambool heading towards Colac Ph: (03) 5567 6260
- Visit the historic town of Koroit, near the Tower Hill State Game Park.
- Explore the town's many quaint shops housed in Edwardian and Victorian era buildings.
- Stroll through the Botanic Gardens, admire the Dragons Blood tree and relax by making use of the picnic and barbecue areas.
- Have a drink or meal at the Koroit Hotel, an old fashioned two-storey pub.

COMING & GOING
- Warrnambool to Port Campbell 66km
- Warrnambool to Port Fairy 29km

Manor Gums is a quality and unique retreat surrounded by tall majestic gums and birdlife. Private self contained suites, generous breakfast basket, spa, BBQ and fires.

Manor Gums

170 Shadys Lane, Mailors Flat, Warrnambool, 3275
Ph: (03) 5565 4410 Fax: (03) 5565 4409
manorgum@hotkey.net.au
www.travel.to/manorgums

VOLCANO, WHALES & SHIPWRECKS

FLAGSTAFF HILL IN WARRNAMBOOL

Warrnambool is famous for its whales. From May/Jun to Sept female southern right whales use the area around Logans Beach as a nursery where they bear their calves. At other times the whales' range between 40º and 55ºS.

WHALES

Southern right whales, so named because they were considered the 'right' whales to hunt, were at one point hunted almost to extinction. These spectacular mammals grow to an average of 15m and 50 tonnes, and are distinguished by their smooth black heads and absence of a dorsal fin.

The birthing cycle for whales is every two-to-three years and their pregnancy is of roughly similar duration to that of humans. They suckle their young from a milk gland beneath the mother's body, vaguely reminiscent again of the human family, perhaps part of their fascination to us.

You might not always be able to spot them on your visit; check at the visitor information centre for news of recent sightings. If they are around, go (probably with many other tourists) to the whale-watching platform at the end of Logans Beach Rd. Leave time for multiple visits, as they cannot be booked to meet the schedules of tourists.

TOWER HILL

Ever wondered what an extinct volcano looks like? Tower Hill was created in an eruption 30 000 years ago. The deep crater so formed became a lake with creeks and islands. However, Tower Hill was denuded by white settlers with its wildlife all but disappearing. In a bid to curb the destruction, Tower Hill was declared Victoria's first National Park in 1892. Revegetation began in 1952, based largely on the intricate paintings of Eugene Von Guerard (commissioned in 1855) identifying various original plant species. Around 300 000 trees have now been planted. Tower Hill became a State Game Park in 1962.

Today the park features a diverse range of native wildlife, including kangaroos, koalas, emus, echidnas and possums, not to mention the bird life. The Parks Victoria website, www.parkweb.vic.gov.au, is a good place to find additional information.

Another impressive feature of the reserve is the Natural History Centre When: 9am–12.30pm Mon–Fri, 10am–3.30pm weekends and public holidays. The centre has displays about the area's geological history and the revegetation program. This centre is run by the Worn Gundidj Aboriginal Co-operative.

WHALE WATCHING IN WARRNAMBOOL

There are five self-guided short walks around the reserve taking from 30min to an hour. While you're in the area, pop in to the nearby town of Koroit (*see* Breaks and Detours p.97)

FLAGSTAFF HILL/ SHIPWRECKED
If you've been to Sovereign Hill, the goldrush attraction in the central Victorian city of Ballarat, you will understand that re-creating towns from a previous era can be one of the best ways of enabling people to engage with the past.

Flagstaff Hill operates on a similar premise, which is instead of walking through a re-created 19th-century gold-mining town, visitors walk through a colonial-era port town. There is a quaint church, a saloon-type pub, a blacksmith's shop and many other essential facilities of the time.

Upon admission, view the 10min video in the theatrette. The video's narration is read from the diary of a man who travelled to Victoria in the 1880s. It explains the claustrophobia, boredom, tasteless food and exposure to the elements suffered by ship passengers, as well as the social attitudes of the time. From there you'll head into the maritime museum, which reminds us that the experience of long-distance seafaring was one that most early Australians endured. The Museum contains an array of genuine relics from shipwrecks, including the famous earthenware peacock from the *Loch Ard*. This museum is changing with the times. The hi-tech sound and laser extravaganza *Shipwrecked* depicts the story, both tragic and heroic, of the passengers of the *Loch Ard,* the 3-masted, square-rigged sailing ship that sank in 1878 off the coast between Port Campbell and Warrnambool leaving only two survivors When: screens nightly at different times throughout the year, bookings essential Ph: 1800 556 111

The Flagstaff Hill complex also houses the Warrnambool Visitor Information Centre, a stylish restaurant, Pippies on the Bay (*see* Food and Wine p.96), both of which offer impressive hilltop views of the old-style village and the bay. The area around Warrnambool is known as the Shipwreck Coast, and with good reason. Find out why at the complex When: 9am–5pm daily Ph: (03) 5559 4600 @: flagstaffhill@warrnambool.vic.gov.au Web: www.flagstaffhill.com

SHIPWRECK HERITAGE AT FLAGSTAFF HILL WARRNAMBOOL

HIGHLIGHTS BETWEEN WARRNAMBOOL AND PORT FAIRY

The short drive between Warrnambool and Port Fairy is rewarding, with whales to spy in winter and the natural beauty of the coastline to appreciate year-round. But travelling a more circuitous route inland via quaint towns like Koroit, Woolsthorpe, Hawkesdale and Kirkstall will add a very different dimension to your journey.

MUST SEE

- Koroit is a quaint and historic town 18km north-east of Port Fairy about halfway to Warrnambool. Stroll through the beautiful Koroit Botanic Gardens which feature a Dragons Blood tree plus picnic and barbecue areas. Follow the heritage trail through the town centre and learn the history of Koroit's old buildings. Experience a spectrum of sights and sounds at the Koroit Irish Festival. Held each year in late April or early May, its mix of social and musical mix aims to please all comers.
- The Murray Goulburn Co-operative is the town's largest employer. Its fleet of 16 tankers takes milk from about 450 local farms to process more than 400 million litres a year.

WORTH VISITING

- Tall tales and true flow like cold beer in Victoria's legendary country pubs, and one of the best ways to experience them, and enjoy some hearty hospitality is by taking the Great Southwest Pub Trail. Soak up the ambience and charm of some of the region's 21 premier watering holes, many of which have looked after travellers for more than 100 years.
  Ph: 1300 739 663
  Web: www.southwestpubtrail.com
- Pubs to visit on the trail include:
  Boggy Creek Pub: Historic limestone hotel on the banks of the Curdies River, meals and accommodation available all week.
  Where: 1636 Boggy Creek Rd, Curdievale
  Ph: (03) 5566 5121
- Shamrock Hotel: cold beer, great meals in the bar, lounge or function room perfect for 21st celebrations or just a night out
  Where: 111 Drummond St, Dennington
  Ph: (03) 5562 5725
- Commercial Hotel: offers family feasts and the coldest beer in the west
  Where: 180 Commercial Rd, Koroit
  Ph: (03) 5565 8510
- Mickey Bourke's Hotel: an historic Irish hotel with a big welcoming archway. Enjoy Guinness on tap plus B&B style accommodation with four poster beds and cosy open fires Where: 101 Commercial Rd, Koroit Ph: (03) 5565 8201
- Kirkstall Hotel: a great community pub close to Koroit and Tower Hill and open daily Where: Atkinson St, Kirkstall
  Ph: (03) 5565 8440
- National Hotel: further north from Port Fairy, a classic white-painted iron roofed country pub with a shady bull-nosed verandah. It provides great meals on Fri–Sat nights (bookings essential)
  Where: 23 Manifold St, Woolsthorpe
  Ph: (03) 5569 2391
- Hawkesdale Hotel: farther afield again from Port Fairy, but worth the drive just for its atmosphere. It has accommodation and counter meals Fri–Sat nights
  Where: 88 Dawson St, Hawkesdale
  Ph: (03) 5560 7252
- The Caledonian Inn Hotel Motel: Don't let the 'hotel motel' in the name put you off. Otherwise known as 'The Stump' this is Victoria's oldest continually licensed hotel. It is famous for 'stump rump', 900g of prime Western District beef
  Where: 41 Bank St, Port Fairy
  Ph: (03) 5568 1044

CAN DO

- Walks around the Tower Hill crater floor and slopes take in spectacular views of the coastline and fascinating geological information.

NATURAL ATTRACTIONS

- Koroit is at the start of the south-west loop of the Volcanic Discovery Trail, and just north of one of its most significant attractions; Tower Hill State Game Park. It is a volcanic phenomenon called a

KOALA AT TOWER HILL

www.planbooktravel.com

'nested maar' and the largest of its type in Victoria, with a crater 3.2km wide. Tower Hill is estimated to be 25 000 years old. A road circles the rim to the Natural History Centre (designed by architect, Robin Boyd) on the crater floor, which also incorporates a picnic ground with barbecues and lakeside boardwalks.
- Tower Hill is a game reserve and the sheltered crater abounds with birds, kangaroos, emus, koalas and echidnas. Cleared for grazing in the 1800s, Tower Hill became Victoria's first National Park in 1892 and was replanted with 300 000 trees by volunteers in the 1950s.

PORT FAIRY SEASCAPE

HISTORICAL INTERESTS
- The Tower Hill Cemetery is the resting place of many important settlers, including the local pioneer and largest landowner in the district, William Rutledge. The human history of the region dates back much further, when the Peek Whuurong Aboriginal tribe lived in a fertile land forested by casuarinas, manna gums, ferns and plants that thrived in the rich volcanic soil. These earliest inhabitants were tall and lived on a healthy diet of shellfish, kangaroo and plants.
- French explorer, Nicholas Baudin, first sighted Tower Hill in 1802. The name Koroit was taken from Peek Whuurong language and given to the area around Tower Hill by Chief Surveyor for Port Phillip, Robert Hoddle, when he surveyed Port Fairy in 1845. By the early 1840s small pieces of land were cultivated by farmers from the Port Fairy area.
- William Rutledge bought 5120 acres (2072ha) from the Crown in 1843 and encouraged Irish immigrants to become tenant farmers by offering them 14 year leases and incentives to clear the land. The need for food on the goldfields helped give farming communities extra incentive. In 1855, a National School was established at Koroit as part of a township surveyed with allotments for churches and gardens, and by the 1870s Koroit was a flourishing settlement.

RETAIL THERAPY
- Koroit is small, but it has a wide range of antique, arts and crafts shops to explore.

STAYING
- There is a caravan and camping ground next to the Koroit Botanic Gardens and a range of other reasonably priced accommodation choices in and around town.

MORE INFO
- Port Fairy Visitor Information Centre
  When: 9am–5pm daily
  Where: Railway Place, Bank St
  Ph: (03) 5568 2682
- Warrnambool Visitor Information Centre
  When: 9am-5pm daily Where: Flagstaff Hill, Merri St Ph: (03) 5564 7837

GREAT OCEAN ROAD AND GRAMPIANS

Located at 72 Liebig St. Warrnambool, on the eastern end of the Great Ocean Road, Beach Babylon offers an extensive a-la-carte menu featuring steak, seafood, pasta and wood-fired oven pizzas. Licensed and BYO (bottled wine only).

Beach Babylon

260km or 3 hours from Melbourne via the Princes Hwy
400km or 4 – 5 hours from Melbourne via the Great Ocean Road

MAHOGANY SHIP

DUNES BELIEVED BY SOME TO COVER THE REMAINS OF THE MAHOGANY SHIP

When the sands blew in over the dunes between Port Fairy and Warrnambool in the 1880s, they created a mystery about what lay under that sand on Victoria's south-west coast.

Was it a Portuguese caravel? Maybe a Dutch East Indiaman? Or, even a Chinese junk from 600 years ago? Or maybe it was just an ordinary whale boat or sealing lighter wrecked on the windswept coast in the early years of settlement?

Recently, however, speculation about the mystery of the fabled wreck of the Mahogany Ship deepened when carbon dating of hand-carved wood dug from under the Warrnambool sands by one searcher proved it to be about 3000 years old. Suddenly the possibilities seemed staggering. The very history of Australia might need to be rewritten.

THE LEGEND

All that's known is that under the sand lies, or lay, the remnants of a mystery vessel of a mahogany or cedar-like dark timber — not planked like most but constructed of panels. From about 1836 to the 1880s, the wreck was a familiar sight to the few who roamed this piece of wild isolated coast. Estimated at 60 to 200 tons, the Mahogany Ship, as it was soon dubbed was first known locally as 'the old wreck' or 'The Stranger', 'and even in the early 1840s it was partly covered in sand.

The editor of the *Warrnambool Examiner*, Richard Osburne, claimed to have seen her several times while riding from Warrnambool to Port Fairy in the late 1840s, as did the former Port Fairy Harbour Master, Captain Mills, rated the most reliable witness. But what no-one did exactly was record its position, except for the vague agreement that she was stranded 'well in among the hummocks', 300 or 400 yards above the high water mark.

By the 1880s, when sand had fully covered the wreck, many of her timbers, had been taken away or burnt, and her deck was missing. And by 1881, when Joseph Archibald, the curator of the Warrnambool museum, tried to find the wreck for a paper being presented to the Geographical Society, it could not be located. Later searches met similar failure. Recently, however, two separate teams of sleuths have sent off pieces of wood recovered along this coast for investigation and carbon dating and that is what's producing all of the excitement. It's even spread to China, with TV and radio crews becoming a familiar sight along the sands, following up the theory that, Aborigines aside, the Chinese discovered Australia. Meanwhile, Warrnambool is still the regular destination for many Portuguese, believers of the theory that the Mahogany ship is in fact theirs, wrecked here and part of a three-ship secret charting of eastern Australia in 1552.

The beauty, and frustration, of the Mahogany Ship is that it remains a puzzle. You can select your own slant on history as have the lawyer, the cray fisherman and the researcher.

THE LAWYER

Melbourne lawyer Mark Rawson has been enthralled by the legend since he was a kid. An amateur historian and archeologist, he and colleagues have laboriously put past witnesses to the ship's location on the stand, examining their stories as if witness statements.

Their big breakthrough came when their self-funded probing of the sands revealed, from an old inlet near Warrnambool, 50 to 60 small pieces of red, obviously hand-cut olive timber. Shaped as if plugs, they are like those used to plug the timbers of ancient ships.

Tests on two separate samples by the Australian Nuclear Science and Technology Organisation's Sydney laboratory revealed that the plugs could be 3000 years old. Rawson had previously put the age of the plugs at 600, or perhaps, 1400 years.

Found about 10.5m down in 'black ooze' in a drained swamp far closer to Warrnambool than most have dug before, the plugs are like those used around the Mediterranean but also used by ancient Indian vessels.

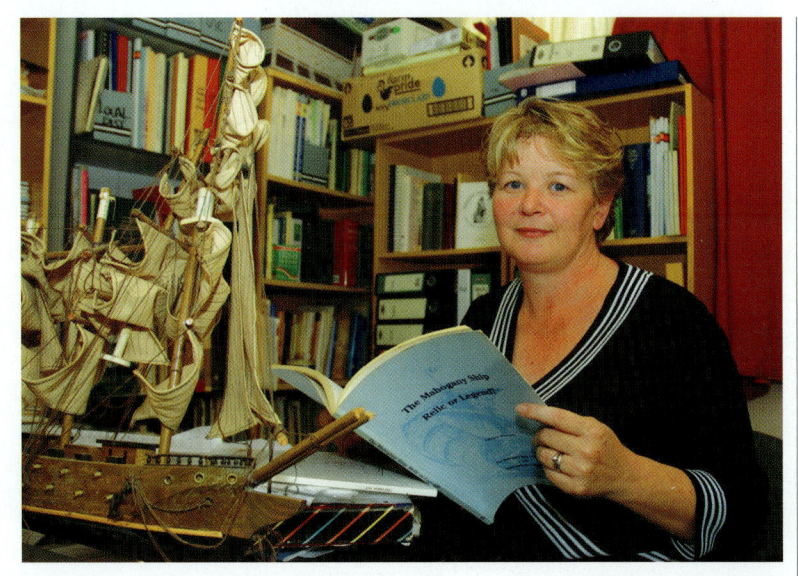

JENNY WILLIAMS FAWCETT

Now Rawson is putting his money 'on the fact that it may be older than Spanish or Portuguese. It may be Chinese, but not necessarily a Chinese-built ship, but, believe it or not, possibly an Indian built ship commissioned by the Chinese,' he speculates. But others are not so sure, suggesting more testing of the timber is needed, and that olive might have been mistaken for Australian native timbers or, even, driftwood.

THE CRAY FISHERMAN

Cray fisherman Andrew Robinson suspects he knows exactly where the Mahogany Ship is located. Modern nautical gadgetry, including Global Positioning Satellite (GPS) navigation, he claims, pinpoint the wreck as being under a 18m dune several kilometres from Warrnambool.

In 2003, he pulled from the sand near his target dune two lengths of wood, one which mysteriously bore a carved initial, either a W or M. When analysis proved the timber to be rare *Alniphyllum fortunei*, or Fortunes China Bells, often used for decking in Asian vessels, he became excited. Might this have been from the wreck? Could this be the proof of Chinese claims that it discovered Australia? Alas, no. Carbon dating showed it to be just 140 years old.

But he is undeterred, stressing that an overlay of his angles and landmarks perfectly match the letter cut into the larger of the two pieces of timber he found. 'Somebody has done that, and that somebody knows more than anybody,' says the seaman in true Treasure Island fashion. 'I don't know why – but they've put that mark in the timber. The whole thing is pointing into one very tight area.'

He suspects the ship, or something sizeable, is under the enormous dune. 'It's got that smell about it and I'm going to keep going no matter what,' he promises.

THE RESEARCHER

Bunkum, says local historian Jenny Williams Fawcett, of theories that the Mahogany ship is Portuguese or Chinese, or even earlier. Her money, based on a decade of painstaking research, tirelessly following up early reports, is that it's likely British or Australian, maybe a colonial vessel forced ashore by the south-east gales that have littered this shoreline with wrecks.

One theory Williams Fawcett advances is that it's a locally-built vessel, made on Kangaroo island of a red timber at the start of the 19th century by the crew of one of the first American ships in Australia. Used as a tender in the sealing industry, it regularly sailed around Bass Strait islands and to Sydney but in 1805 disappeared at sea with more than 12 men.

Of theories put forward by others, this modern sleuth claims much of the Mahogany Ship story was distorted by an earlier resident of the area with the knack for spinning a good yarn. His fabricated 19th century accounts, she laments, have misled searchers and researchers for decades.

Williams Fawcett's research leaves the story of Australia's discovery unchanged. But if any one of the Portuguese, Indian or Chinese theories is proved correct, Australia's history will demand a major rewrite.

Visitors can take the 23km Mahogany Ship Walking Track from Port Fairy to Warrnambool. It passes possible wreck sites and individual sections are easily accessed.

PLAQUE HONOURING PORTUGUESE NAVIGATORS

PORT FAIRY

www.planbooktravel.com

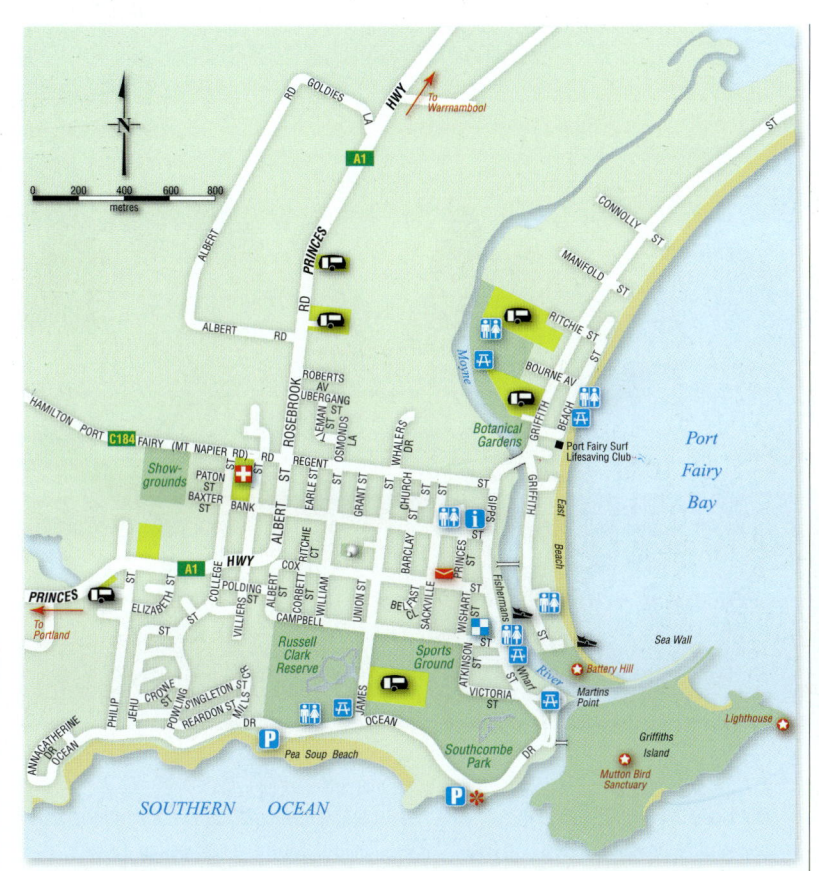

This former whaling port on the estuary of the Moyne River has been transformed into one of Victoria's most captivating and historic holiday resorts. Bordered by both river and ocean, it is also home to a large fishing fleet and is well known for crayfish and abalone fishing. But the town's particular claim to fame is the famous Port Fairy Folk Festival, an annual gathering of music lovers from around the world.

In many ways, Port Fairy has changed little in a century or more. Quaint whitewashed cottages still line its broad streets and you can still buy the 'catch of the day' fresh from the fishing boats at the wharf.

East and South Beaches are popular swimming spots and historic inns, hostels and many of the former whalers' cottages have been sympathetically converted into quality restaurants and accommodation.

POPULATION:
2850

MUST SEE
- The world-famous Port Fairy Folk Festival bursts into song over the Labour Day long weekend in March, drawing thousands of people into the tiny town. The four-day event features Australian and overseas acts playing a wide selection of world, roots and acoustic music. From small beginnings in 1977, the festival is now so popular that even tent sites at the caravan parks are sought after. Tickets can sell out within a day when bookings open in November so we suggest you get in quickly Ph: (03) 5568 2682 (festival information and bookings).
- Other happening events include the six-week Moyneyana Festival in summer which celebrates outdoor activities, including a raft race on the Moyne River, and reaches its peak with the Moyneyana New Year's Eve Procession. In Easter the annual Queenscliff to Port Fairy yacht race ends here with yet another big party.

WORTH VISITING
- Griffiths Island is poised between the ocean and Port Fairy Bay and linked to the town by a long causeway. The island is home to a mutton-bird rookery and between Sept and Apr you can watch them roost at dusk from a specially constructed lookout. Every year around September the mutton birds arrive for nesting and stay until Apr when the adults begin their Pacific migration. Younger birds set off after the adults but still manage to find their way.
- At the eastern tip of Griffiths Island is the historic Port Fairy Lighthouse. Built by Scottish masons in 1859, this 11m bluestone tower presides over the rugged rocky shore where the Southern Ocean breaks.

CAN DO
- Port Fairy Golf Club is a beautiful 18-hole course set on the ocean's edge. The greens and fairways are as picturesque as the ocean views beside them, and the clubhouse surveying the course is ideal for recapping your game over a cool drink
When: daily Ph: (03) 5568 2866 (for tee-off times and bookings)
Web: www.portfairygolf.com.au

PORT FAIRY

MOORINGS AT PORT FAIRY

PORT FAIRY

- Riding a bike around town is a great way to take in the natural beauty and heritage sights up close. Or perhaps you'd prefer to go fly a kite in the park. Both bikes and kites are available for hire at the Kite House Ph: (03) 5568 2782
- Take a morning camel ride along East Beach or during the afternoon at George Dodds Reserve near Martins Point When: 26 Dec–24 Jan

  Camel rides coincide with the Moyneyana Festival, Moyneyana meaning 'having fun along the river', that includes children's fun days, Dr Bunn's Travelling Circus and a variety of other family events. There is a New Year's Eve parade with live music and fireworks at midnight. When: The festival runs 26 Dec–26 Jan.
- Experience the thrill of surfing with tuition from qualified coaches at Easyrider Surf School. This tourism award-winning business provides safe fun in the waves on soft foam surfboards and is suitable for all ages Ph: 0418 328 747 Web: www.easyridersurfschool.com.au
- A more leisurely way to see the sea is by boat cruise. Experience Lady Julia Percy Island, appreciate Port Fairy from the bay, or go on a fishing expedition with Port Fairy Boat Charter. Boats leave daily from the wharf Ph: (03) 5568 1480 Web: www.myportfairy.com/boatcharter

THE PORT FAIRY FOLK FESTIVAL

PORT FAIRY FOLK FESTIVAL

One of the top five folk music festivals in the world, the Port Fairy Folk Festival is a fabulous celebration of culture and music through the diverse styles that come under the banner of 'folk' music — everything from country, Celtic, jazz, blues and bluegrass to contemporary, acoustic, rock and world music. Held in early March each year for four days over the Labour Day long weekend, it showcases major international and national artists in back-to-back performances. There are also sessions, choirs, theme concerts, workshops, classes and theatre.

Established in 1977, the festival has grown to an unprecedented extent, attracting more than 60 000 people each year to its unique blend of family and community experiences. Such success has been rewarded with numerous tourism awards, so many that the festival was inducted into the *Australian Tourism Hall Of Fame* in 1995.

Between 1999 and 2005 the festival has consistently sold out four months in advance, with more than 95 percent of visitors keen to come back the next year. Many of these enthusiastic attendees stay for more than the four-day event, their heads and hearts still reeling from a whirlwind of exciting cultural concerts, stories, markets, camping experiences, dancing, singing, reunions with old friends and the chance to make new ones.

The festival magically transforms the little fishing village of Port Fairy with more than just music. There are the parades, fairs, markets, busking, children's events and street theatre — and all that is simply what is happening as part of its Free Festival of the Streets which takes place alongside five main concerts in the ticketed arena.

Other festival highlights and events include the festival craft fair, markets and a scrumptious food festival, plus a fascinating instrument-maker's exhibition, energetic buskers, theatre, music sessions, sing-alongs, special awards, street performances and poets' breakfasts. The main festival arena contains five stages, a children's folk circus, wine bar, Guinness club, Lighthouse Cafe, workshop stages, pavilion, food festival and market, and craft stalls. The arena is surrounded by other interesting venues including churches, halls, street stages, parks, markets, pubs and clubs.

The Port Fairy Folk Festival is organised and presented by the Port Fairy Folk Festival Committee with the help and hospitality of local residents, businesses and the shire, as well as many local community clubs, organisations and an army of dedicated volunteers called the Friends of the Festival. For more information and bookings contact the Port Fairy Visitor Information Centre or visit the festival website Ph: (03) 5568 2682 Web: www.portfairyfolkfestival.com

PORT FAIRY

HISTORICAL INTERESTS

- One of Victoria's oldest towns, Port Fairy features more than 50 National Trust-classified stone cottages and bluestone buildings. Stroll around 30 of these wonderful old buildings on the Port Fairy Heritage Walk. Pick up a free leaflet for this self-guided tour from the Port Fairy Visitor Information Centre.
- Port Fairy was fortified against a feared Russian invasion in the 1860s and three cannons commemorate this at Battery Point, an old fort and signal station at the mouth of the Moyne River. For more heritage details visit the History Centre located in the old Court House on Gipps St by the river. It displays costumes, historic photographs, shipwreck relics and other items relating to the town's pioneering history When: Wed, Sat–Sun 2–5pm, daily during school holidays and long weekends Ph: (03) 5568 2263

FOOD & DRINK

- There are ample offerings for breakfast lunch and dinner in Port Fairy. The following is an indication of what's on offer; Lunch cafe in the old Borough Chambers has appetising food and ambience When: Wed–Sun 9am–5pm, dinner Fri–Sun, with extended hours during peak seasons Where: 20 Bank St. Rebecca's cafe serves breakfasts, light lunches, cakes and good coffee. Indulge in delicious home-made ice-cream next door Where: 70 Sackville St.
- Culpepper's is a well stocked health food shop that serves Devonshire teas and light meals Where: 24 Bank St, next to the Port Fairy Visitor Information Centre.
- For high-end dining, try the licensed restaurant at the Stag Restaurant at Seacombe House Motor Inn When: 6.30–9.30pm daily in summer (ring to check other times) Where: 22 Sackville St (Seacombe House) Ph: (03) 5568 3058 or 5568 1077 (bookings essential).
- One of the best places to drink is the Caledonian Inn, better know to locals as 'The Stump'. Established in 1844, it is the oldest continuously licensed pub in Victoria Where: cnr Banks and James Sts

STAYING

- Port Fairy's village atmosphere and excellent accommodation options, plus cosy pubs, tearooms and restaurants, makes it an ideal place to stay. Choices extend from luxury apartments and quality motels to heritage cottages and budget caravan/camping. Among the many charming colonial cottages and B&Bs are Whalers Cottages (cnr Whalers Dr and Regent St), Cottages of the Port (96 Gipps St) and Lough Cottage (216 Griffith St). For full details on all Port Fairy accommodation (including Port Fairy's six caravan parks) contact the Port Fairy Visitor Information Centre. When: 9am–5pm daily, shorter hours in winter Where: Railway Pl on Bank St Ph: (03) 5568 2682 @: vic@moyne.vic.gov.au

MORE INFO

- Visitor information centre When: 9am–5pm daily Where: Railway Place, Bank St Ph: (03) 5568 2682 Web: www.moyne.vic.gov.au, or www.myportfairy.com

COMING & GOING

- Port Fairy to Portland 73km
- Port Fairy to Warrnambool 29km

PORT FAIRY LIGHTHOUSE

GREAT OCEAN ROAD AND GRAMPIANS

SOUTHERN RIGHT WHALE

MAMMALS AND MUTTON BIRDS

Encountering whales and seals along this section of the southern coast is an extra special reward. Each of these amazing marine mammal is unique and makes the GOR scenery all the more captivating. But less than 70 years ago they provided a very different kind of prize. Whales and seals were hunted in their thousands for over 100 years along this coastline, until the practice was finally banned in 1935. From the late 1820s to the early 1830s, whaling and sealing were the primary industries on the south coast of Victoria, particularly in places like Port Fairy and Portland.

The whalers' primary target was the southern right whale, named because early whalers considered it the 'right' species of whale to hunt. Predominantly found in southern waters, southern right whales were easy targets because they swam slowly and close to shore, they floated when harpooned and provided large quantities of oil and whalebone. These gentle giants were hunted almost to extinction but since the ban on whaling their numbers have steadily increased. Today many southern right whales visit the coast each winter to calve in the waters off Logans Beach in Warrnambool.

PORTLAND WHALING:

Several early explorers sighted, named and charted the area around Portland, including Lieutenant James Grant (who named Portland Bay after the Duke of Portland in 1800), the French explorer Captain Nicolas Baudin, and Captain Matthew Flinders; but the first settlement in the region was made by sealers and whalers. In 1829 Captain William Dutton established a shore-based whaling station at a time when Portland Bay was considered one of the best whaling grounds in the world and annual catches regularly in the hundreds.

PORT FAIRY WHALING:

First sighted from Bass Strait by Lieutenant Grant, Port Fairy was one of Victoria's earliest ports and whalers and sealers immediately saw its potential. They hunted here for many years, setting up 'boiling down' cauldrons on the beach close to where whales passed on their annual migration.

A bay whaling station established on an island at the river mouth by Penny and Reiby in 1835 was purchased by early entrepreneur, John Griffiths, and the island now bears his name. By the mid-1840s the supply of southern right whales was exhausted and the whaling station closed, but so many whales were slaughtered in those years that the East Beach of the island was strewn with their enormous bones. Years later these were collected, ground into powder and used as fertiliser.

PORT FAIRY MUTTON BIRDS AND SEALS:

Griffiths Island near Port Fairy is now a sanctuary for the short-tailed shearwater, or mutton bird. They nest on the island Sept–Apr after migrating from North America. Remarkably, each bird returns each year to the same burrow. For many years these predictable birds were hunted for food by the early pioneers and their numbers decimated. Today they are at full strength, and watching tens of thousands of them arrive each year is a spectacular sight. Walk around the island and observe the mutton birds' nests from a viewing platform, which also affords great views of the coast and river. More than 20 000 Australian fur seals live on tiny Lady Julia Percy Island, a flat-topped volcanic protrusion 9km off the coast near Port Fairy. The seals make their homes in caves and along its rocky beaches. Charters to the island are conducted from Port Fairy wharf but landing on the island requires a permit from Parks Victoria.

HIGHLIGHTS BETWEEN PORT FAIRY AND PORTLAND

SOUTHERN RIGHT WHALE NEAR WARRNAMBOOL

The long sweep of the Great Ocean Road connecting Port Fairy and Portland follows the curve of Portland Bay, passing the small hamlets of Yambuk, Tyrendarra and Narrawong along the way. Keep an eye out for waterspouts and splashes erupting from the ocean. Each are tell-tale signs that southern right whales are out there, particularly May/Jun–Sept. But the coast road isn't the only way to get there.

You can divert inland and experience the natural splendour of Mt Eccles National Park. While this lengthens the journey considerably, visiting this geological phenomenon about 45km north-west of Port Fairy is a must.

MUST SEE
- The 6120ha Mt Eccles National Park is located at the western edge of the volcanic plains that extend north to Hamilton and Ararat and east all the way to Melbourne. About 20 000 years ago, volcanic eruptions ripped open the earth's crust, disgorging thousands of tonnes of molten lava to form Mt Eccles and the surrounding landscape.
- Today the lava is covered with fertile heathland and manna gum forests, but numerous volcanic features are still visible, including lava flows, lava caves, scoria cones and crater lakes. The 700m-long Lake Surprise is contained within three main craters and replenished by underground springs.

CAN DO
- If you're prepared to stretch your legs, there are ample fascinating activities in and around the park, like exploring a lava cave, swimming in the crater of a volcano and koala spotting.
- Walk around the rim then descend into the crater and follow the shoreline of the lake. Take the rough track along the lava canal and see the broken basalt of the old lava flows.
- Visit the Byaduk Caves, one of the most extensive and accessible sets of lava caves in Australia. Only one cave is open to the public. Contact the park ranger to arrange access.
- Climb the most recently active volcano in Victoria, Mt Napier, in nearby Mt Napier State Park. Stand on the edge of its volcanic cone and survey views that extend from the Grampians to the ocean.

NATURAL ATTRACTIONS
- The impressive protuberances of the Crags are only 12km west along the GOR outside Port Fairy. The Crags offer panoramic views along Port Fairy's coastline as well as uninterrupted views of Lady Julia Percy Island. This rugged stretch of coastline is in striking contrast to the gentle swimming beaches and bays of Port Fairy.
- The most common species of trees and plants in the park are manna gum, blackwood and austral bracken, alongside less prevalent cherry balart trees, everlasting poa grass, native elderberry, kangaroo apple and correas.
- Wildlife is prolific, including koalas, sugar and yellow-bellied gliders, possums, eastern grey kangaroos, quolls, brush-tailed phascogales and dusky and swamp antechinus. More than 60 bird species have been recorded in the park, including the grey thrush, peregrine falcon, parrots, wrens, ducks and coots.

SLEEPING KOALA, MT ECCLES

More Info: For further details on Mt Eccles National Park contact Parks Victoria Ph: 13 19 63
Web: www.parkweb.vic.gov.au

HISTORICAL INTERESTS

- The volcanic eruptions that began around Mt Eccles about 20 000 years ago continued for 12 000 years, with the last eruption occurring about 8000 years ago. Aboriginal tribes occupied two areas around Mt Eccles, south of the park at Lake Gorrie and at Lake Condah to the west. They constructed stone huts in both areas and stone fish traps at Lake Condah, and lived on fish, native plants and animals. They were permanent residents in the region until European settlement slowly pushed them out.
- Mt Eccles became a public purposes (picnic) reserve in 1926. The 35ha park was managed by a local committee that built the existing picnic shelter and the Lake Surprise track. After WWII, the Shire of Minhamite managed the park until it became a National Park in 1960. In 1968, 400ha was added by incorporating a section of the Stones Flora and Faunal Reserve to the west of Mt Eccles. When the rest of the reserve was added in 1985, Mt Eccles National Park increased to its present size to encompass most of the lava flow from Mt Eccles.

STAYING

- The camping grounds at Mt Eccles National Park provide basic facilities including fireplaces, tables, hot showers and toilets. There are also sites available for large groups and people with disabilities. Camping fees apply and bookings are required in peak periods. The picnic ground has fireplaces, tables, toilets, a picnic shelter and an information centre.

LAVA CAVES, MT ECCLES NATIONAL PARK

PORTLAND